ULTIMA
CHEESE-MAKING
COOKBOOK

50 EASY & FUN RECIPES
FOR A HEALTHY LIFESTYLE

FRANK HEARN

TABLE OF CONTENTS

INTRODUCTION

Welcome to cheese making!

Everybody loves cheese but what really is it and why dont we make it more often at home.Cheese is a dairy product derived from milk that is produced in a wide range of flavors, textures, and forms by coagulation of the milk protein casein. It comprises proteins and fat from milk, usually the milk of cows, buffalo, goats, or sheep.
Most homemade cheese is made from milk, bacteria and rennet. Cheese can be made from almost any kind of milk including cow, goat, sheep, and skim, whole, raw, pasteurized and powdered.

Home cheese making differs from commercial cheese making in scale and in the need to produce exact duplicate products day after day for retail markets. Commercial cheese makers use the same ingredients as home cheese makers, but they must obtain local certifications and follow strict regulations. If you would like to sell your cheese, it's important you start by making simple cheese.

What makes each cheese so different when different tytpes of cheese use the same ingredients? At first glance, it may seem that different types of cheese are made the same way. However, the differences in cheese come from very slight variations in the process. Cheddar and Colby, for example, are very similar as they start out, but Colby has a step where water is added to the curds, causing it to a higher moisture cheese than Cheddar.

Some other factors that play a role in the final cheese include the amount of culture, ripening time, amount of rennet, size of the curds, how long and high the milk is heated, the length of time curds are stirred, and how the whey is removed. Minor changes in any of these areas can make a dramatic difference in the final cheese.

The yield of cheese from one gallon of milk is approximately one pound for the hard cheese and two pounds for the soft cheese.

When buying cheese making supplies it is a good idea to find a Cheese Making Recipe first, then start making a list of the ingredients and equipment you will need to make your cheese.

COATED & RUBBED CHEESES

1. Brin d'Amour

MAKES 1 pound

- 2 quarts pasteurized goat's milk
- 2 quarts pasteurized whole cow's milk
- ¼ teaspoon MA 4001 powdered mesophilic starter culture
- 1 teaspoon calcium chloride diluted in ¼ cup cool nonchlorinated water
- 1 teaspoon liquid rennet diluted in ¼ cup cool nonchlorinated water

- 2 teaspoons   ne sea salt
- 1½ teaspoons dried thyme
- 1½ teaspoons dried oregano
- 1½ teaspoons dried savory
- 1½ teaspoons herbes de Provence

- 3 tablespoons dried rosemary
- 1 teaspoon paprika
- 1 teaspoon whole coriander seeds
- 1 teaspoon whole mixed peppercorns
- 1 teaspoon whole juniper berries
- 2 teaspoons olive oil

1. In a nonreactive 6-quart stockpot, heat the milks over low heat to 86°F; this should take about 15 minutes. Turn off the heat.

2. Sprinkle the starter over the milk and let it rehydrate for 5 minutes. Mix well using a whisk in an up-and-down motion. Add the calcium chloride and gently whisk in, and then add the rennet in the same way.

3. Cover and maintain 72°F, allowing the milk to ripen for 8 hours, or until the curds form one large mass the consistency of thick yogurt and clear whey is oating around the sides of the pot. Check the curds for a clean break. If the cut edge is clean, the curds are ready.

4. Place a strainer over a bowl or bucket large enough to capture the whey. Line it with damp butter muslin. Gently cut ½-inch-thick slices of the curds using a ladle or skimmer and gently ladle the slices into the strainer. Gently toss the curds with 1 teaspoon of the salt, then tie the muslin into a draining sack and hang to let drain at room temperature for 6 to 10 hours, until the whey stops dripping.

5. The longer the curds drain, the drier the nished cheese will be. Alternatively, you can drain the curds by hanging for 45 minutes, then moving the sack to a 4-inch Camembert mold without a bottom, placed on a draining rack. Drain and ripen in the mold for 6 to 10 hours, ipping the curds once during the draining process and sprinkling the remaining 1 teaspoon salt over the surface of the cheese.

6. If not using the mold for the nal shape, transfer the sack to a clean work surface and roll the curds into a ball, then atten slightly with your hands. Open the sack and sprinkle the remaining 1 teaspoon salt over the cheese and lightly rub it into the surface. Set the cheese on a draining rack at room temperature for 8 hours to allow the salt to be absorbed into the cheese and excess moisture to be released. Continue to air-dry for a total of 24 hours, or until the surface is dry.

7. Combine the herbs and spices in a small bowl. Pat the cheese dry of any moisture, then rub thoroughly with the olive oil. Spread a layer of the herb mixture on a sheet of parchment or waxed paper and roll the cheese in the mixture to coat, then gently press the herbs so they stick to the surface of the cheese. Reserve the unused herbs.

8. Cover the cheese with plastic wrap and place in a ripening box at 50°F to 55°F and 80 to 85 percent humidity for 3 days. Remove the plastic wrap, coat with more herbs if needed, and place in a ripening box at 50°F to 55°F for 27 more days. The cheese will be ready to eat at this point or can be aged for another month.

2. Cocoa-Rubbed Dry Jack Cheese

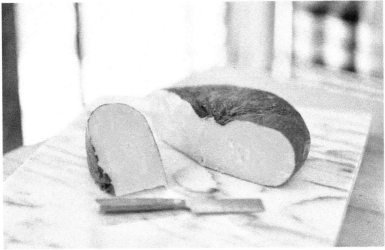

MAKES 2 pounds

- 2 gallons pasteurized whole cow's milk
- 1 teaspoon MA 4001 powdered mesophilic starter culture
- 1 teaspoon calcium chloride diluted in ¼ cup cool nonchlorinated water
- 1 teaspoon liquid rennet diluted in ¼ cup cool nonchlorinated water
- Kosher salt (preferably Diamond Crystal brand) or cheese salt
- 2 tablespoons cocoa powder
- 2 teaspoons instant espresso
- 1½ teaspoons Vnely ground black pepper
- 4½ teaspoons olive oil

1. In a nonreactive 10-quart stockpot, heat the milk over low heat to 86°F; this should take about 15 minutes. Turn o the heat.

2.   Sprinkle the starter over the milk and let it rehydrate for 5 minutes. Mix well using a whisk in an up-and-down motion. Cover and maintain 86°F, allowing the milk to ripen for 1 hour. Add the calcium chloride and gently whisk in for 1 minute. Add the rennet and gently whisk in for 1 minute. Cover and let sit, maintaining 86°F for 30 to 45 minutes, or until the curds give a clean break.

3.   Still maintaining 86°F, cut the curds into ¾-inch pieces and let sit for 5 minutes. Over low heat, slowly bring the curds to 102°F over 40 minutes, stirring continuously to keep the curds from matting together. The curds will release whey, Xrm up slightly, and shrink to the size of dried beans. Maintain 102°F and let the curds rest undisturbed for 30 minutes; they will sink to the bottom.

4.   Ladle out enough whey to expose the curds. Still holding the temperature, stir continuously for 15 to 20 minutes, or until the curds are matted and cling together when pressed in your hand.

5.   Place a strainer over a bowl or bucket large enough to capture the whey. Line it with damp butter muslin and ladle the curds into it Let drain for 5 minutes, then sprinkle in 1 tablespoon of salt and gently and thoroughly mix with your hands.

6.   Draw the ends of the cloth together and twist to form a ball to help squeeze out the excess moisture. Roll the ball on a Pat surface to release more whey. Tie oU the top of the cloth sack, press it with your hands to atten

slightly, and place it on a cutting board sitting on top of a draining rack. Place a second cutting board on top of the Iattened sack and set an 8-pound weight directly over the cheese. Press at 75°F to 85°F for 6 hours for moist Jack or 8 hours for drier Jack.

7. Remove the cheese from the sack and pat dry. Rub with 1 tablespoon of salt and place on a draining rack to air-dry for 8 hours.

8. Make 3 quarts of saturated brine (see Brine Chart) and chill to 50°F to 55°F. Place the cheese in the brine and soak at 50°F to 55°F for 8 hours, Kipping it over once during that time. Remove from the brine, pat dry, and air-dry on a rack at room temperature for hours, or until the surface is dry to the touch. Flip once during this drying period.

9. Place the cheese on a cheese mat in a ripening box at 50°F to 55°F and 85 percent humidity for 1 week, Kipping the cheese daily for even ripening.

10. Combine the cocoa, espresso, and pepper in a small bowl. Add the olive oil and stir to combine. Rub one-fourth of the cocoa mixture all over the cheese. Place the cheese on a rack so air circulates all around it, then continue to ripen at 50°F to 55°F overnight. Repeat the rubbing and air-drying process every day for 3 more days, then ripen the cheese at 60°F and 75 percent humidity for 2 months, tipping twice a week.

11. Wrap in cheese paper and refrigerate until ready to eat— up to 10 months or, for a very rich, deep avor, up to 2

years, if you can wait that long! Once opened, the cheese will dry out and harden as time goes on, creating a wonderful grating cheese.

3. Lavender Mist Chèvre

MAKES Six 4-ounce disks

- 1 gallon pasteurized goat's milk
- ¼ teaspoon MA 4001 powdered mesophilic starter culture
- 1 teaspoon calcium chloride diluted in ¼ cup cool nonchlorinated water
- 1 teaspoon liquid rennet diluted in ¼ cup cool nonchlorinated water
- 1 teaspoon Vne sea salt
- ½ teaspoon fennel pollen powder
- ¼ teaspoon ground lavender or lavender buds

1. In a nonreactive 6-quart stockpot, heat the milk over low heat to 86°F; this should take about 15 minutes. Turn off the heat.

2. Sprinkle the starter over the milk and let it rehydrate for 5 minutes. Mix well using a whisk in an up-and-down motion. Add the calcium chloride and gently whisk in, and then whisk in the rennet in the same way. Cover and maintain 72°F, allowing the milk to ripen for 12 hours, or until the curds have formed one large mass the consistency of thick yogurt and clear whey is oating around the sides of the pot.

3. Place a strainer over a bowl or bucket large enough to capture the whey. Line it with damp butter muslin and gently ladle the curds into the strainer. Add ½ teaspoon of the salt and gently toss to combine. Tie the tails of the cloth to make a draining sack and hang to let drain at room temperature for 6 to 12 hours.

4. Remove the cheese from the cloth and shape it into six 4-ounce round disks. Sprinkle the remaining ½ teaspoon salt over the surface of each cheese and lightly rub it into the surface. Set the cheeses on a drying rack at room temperature for 4 hours to allow them to absorb the salt and release excess moisture.

5. Combine the fennel pollen and lavender in a small bowl. Pat the cheeses dry, then place them on a sheet of

parchment or waxed paper and dust all sides with the herb mixture.

6. Place the cheeses on a rack and let sit at room temperature for 1 hour, then wrap each cheese in plastic wrap and refrigerate for at least 3 days to allow the Flavors of the rub to infuse the cheese and up to 10 days.

4. Honey-Rubbed Montasio

MAKES 2 pounds

- 1 gallon pasteurized reduced fat (2 percent) cow's milk
- 1 gallon pasteurized goat's milk
- 1 teaspoon Thermo C powdered thermophilic starter culture
- 1 teaspoon calcium chloride diluted in ¼ cup cool nonchlorinated water
- 1 teaspoon liquid rennet diluted in ¼ cup cool nonchlorinated water
- 3 teaspoons ake sea salt (or Himalayan sea salt)

- Kosher salt (preferably Diamond Crystal brand) or cheese salt for brining
- 3 tablespoons honey

1. In a nonreactive 10-quart pot, heat the milks over low heat to 90°F; this should take about 20 minutes. Turn oD the heat.
2.   Sprinkle the starter over the milk and let it rehydrate for 5 minutes. Mix well using a whisk in an up-and-down motion. Cover and maintain 90°F, allowing the milk to ripen for 45 minutes. Add the calcium chloride and gently whisk in for 1 minute. Add the rennet and gently whisk in for 1 minute. Cover and let sit, maintaining 90°F for 30 to 45 minutes, or until the curds give a clean break.

3.   Cut the curds into ½-inch pieces and let sit undisturbed for 5 minutes. Over low heat, slowly bring the curds to 104°F over 40 minutes, stirring two or three times. Remove from the heat and stir for 15 minutes to release whey and shrink the curds to the size of peanuts.
4. Over low heat, slowly bring the temperature to 112°F over 5 to 7 minutes, stirring the curds to Vrm them up. Once 112°F is reached, remove from the heat, maintain the temperature, and let the curds rest for 20 minutes; they will sink to the bottom.

5.   Ladle oG enough whey to expose the curds. Place a strainer over a bowl or bucket large enough to capture the whey. Line it with damp butter muslin and gently ladle the curds into it. Let drain for 10 minutes, then sprinkle 1½ teaspoons of the sea salt over the curds and gently

but thoroughly toss with your hands. Let drain for 5 more minutes.

6.   Draw the ends of the muslin together to form a ball and twist to help squeeze out the excess moisture. Place the sack on a sanitized cutting board, roll it into a ball, and tie oO the top to secure the curds in a round shape. Place both wrapped curds and cutting board on a draining rack and press down on the curds with your hands to atten slightly.

7.   Smooth out the knot and ties as best you can to create a stable surface for a second cutting board to rest on. Place the second cutting board on top of the cheese; press down to even out the bundle, then cover the whole assembly completely with a kitchen towel. Place an 8-pound weight over the cheese and press for 8 hours or overnight at 75°F to 85°F.

8.   Make 2 quarts of near-saturated brine (see Brine Chart) and chill to 50°F to 55°F. Remove the cheese from the sack and place it in the brine to soak at 50°F to 55°F for 12 hours, ipping it once to brine evenly. Remove the cheese from the brine and pat dry, then place it on a cheese mat or rack to air-dry at room temperature for hours, or until the surface is dry to the touch. Flip once during this time.

9.   Place in a ripening box at 50°F to 55°F and 85 percent humidity and age for 1 week, ipping daily. Then brush with a simple brine solution (see Brine Chart), cooled to 50°F to 55°F, twice a week for 2 weeks.

10.   After 2 weeks, rub the cheese with 1½ tablespoons of the honey to coat, then return it to the ripening box at 50°F to 55°F and 80 percent humidity for 1 week, ipping daily. The honey will form a Plm, preventing the cheese from drying out.

11. After 1 more week, rub with the remaining 1½ tablespoons of honey and then with the remaining 1½ teaspoons of salt.

12. Return the cheese to the ripening box for 2 more weeks, Uipping daily, then vacuum-seal or wrap tightly in plastic wrap to protect the coating, and store refrigerated for 1 month up to 1 year.

5. Rustico Foglie di Noce

a) You'll need 4 to 6 large dried walnut leaves, stemmed, blanched, and patted dry.

b) To best emulate the robust Wavors that come with the use of sheep's milk, a small amount of cream and a bit of lipase powder are added to the goat's and cow's milks.

c) Make the cheese using the Montasio recipe, combining 1 cup of heavy cream with the milks. After adding the culture and before adding the calcium chloride and rennet, add a pinch of lipase powder.

d) Follow the directions through the rst stage of ripening, prior to rubbing with honey (through step 7). Rub the cheese with olive oil, then sprinkle with kosher salt and rub it into the surface. Though it's not traditional, you can rub the cheese with smoked olive oil alternating with unflavored olive oil for a smoky avor. The best smoked olive oil comes from the Smoked Olive, www.thesmokedolive.com.

e) Brush the walnut leaves on both sides with olive oil, then wrap enough leaves around the cheese to cover it fully. Place the cheese in a ripening box at 50°F to 55°F and 75 percent humidity with good air circulation and age for 3 months, Dipping daily for the rest week, then twice a week thereafter.

f) Rub the cheese daily with olive oil. Consume the cheese once it has aged 3 months, or vacuum-seal or wrap in plastic and store refrigerated for another month.

g) When you're ready to serve these cheeses, allow diners to peel away the leaf wrapping on their portion of cheese.

6. Young Époisses

Ingredients

- 500g pack white bread mix
- 100g walnut pieces
- 140g dried apricots , sliced
- 25g poppy seeds , toasted
- 400ml milk
- a little oil , for greasing
- 1 egg , beaten
- 1-2 soft cheeses in boxes, like brie or camembert
- splash of white wine

Method

1. Tip the bread mix into a food processor, add the walnuts and whizz until fully incorporated. Transfer to a bowl and stir in the apricots and most of the poppy seeds.

Warm the milk to hand temperature, then stir into the flour mix with a wooden spoon. Knead in the bowl until smooth. Cover with oiled cling film and leave somewhere warm-ish to rise for 1 hr.

2.   Find a heatproof dish the same size or a bit bigger than your cheese box. Sit it in the middle of a big baking tray.

3.   Shape the risen dough into a long, thin log that will wrap around the dish on the sheet, like a wreath. Press the ends together, loosely cover with oiled cling film and leave to rise for 20-30 mins.

4.   Heat oven to 180C/160C fan/gas 4. Brush the egg all over the loaf, then sprinkle with the remaining poppy seeds. Using kitchen scissors, randomly snip into the dough, to give a spiky finish. Bake for 35-40 mins until golden and crusty, and the bottom sounds hollow when you tap it. Remove the dish from the middle.

5.   To serve, unwrap the cheese and put it back into the box. Stab a few times, add the wine and tie kitchen string around the box to secure it in case the glue comes undone. Sit the cheese in the middle of the bread, without its lid, and bake for 10-15 mins until molten. Serve straight away and, if you like, pop another cheese in the oven so you can finish off the bread when the first cheese box is wiped clean.

BLOOMY-RIND AND SURFACE-RIPENED CHEESES

7. Crème fraîche brie

MAKES One 10- to 12-ounce wheel or two 5- to 6-ounce wheels

- Penicillium candidum mold powder
- Kosher salt (preferably Diamond Crystal brand) or sea salt
- 2 gallon pasteurized whole cow's milk
- 1 teaspoon Meso II powdered mesophilic starter culture
- 1/8 teaspoon Geotrichum candidum
- 15 mold powder

- 1 teaspoon calcium chloride diluted in ¼ cup cool nonchlorinated water
- ½ teaspoon liquid rennet diluted in ¼ cup cool nonchlorinated water
- 1½ cups cultured crème fraîche, homemade or store-bought, at room temperature

1. Twelve hours before starting, combine a pinch of Penicillium candidum, ¼ teaspoon salt, and 2 cups of cool nonchlorinated water in an atomizer or spray bottle. Store at 50°F to 55°F.

2. In a nonreactive 6-quart stockpot, slowly heat the milk to 86°F over low heat; this should take about 15 minutes. Turn off the heat.

3. Sprinkle the starter, ⅛ teaspoon of P. candidum mold powder, and the Geotrichum candidum mold powder over the milk and let rehydrate for 5 minutes. Mix well using a whisk in an up-and-down motion for 20 strokes. Cover and maintain 86°F, letting the milk ripen for 30 minutes. Add the calcium chloride and gently whisk in, then add the rennet in the same way. Cover and let sit, maintaining 86°F for 1½ hours, or until the curds give a clean break.

4. Cut the curds into ½-inch pieces and let sit for 5 minutes to rm up the curds. Using a rubber spatula, gently stir for 5 minutes around the edges of the pot to move the curds around. Let the curds rest for 5 minutes; they will sink to the bottom.

5. Ladle over enough whey to expose the curds. Gently ladle the curds into a colander lined with damp butter muslin and let drain for 10 minutes, or until the whey stops dripping.

6. Place the crème fraîche in a bowl and whisk to soften. Using a rubber spatula, gently fold the crème fraîche into the curds to combine. Let drain for 10 minutes, until any residual liquid has drained out.

7. Set a draining rack over a tray, put a cutting board on the rack and a cheese mat on the board, and, nally, place one 8-inch Brie mold or two 4-inch Camembert molds on the mat. Ladle the curds into the mold or molds and let drain for 2 hours. The curds will reduce to about two-thirds the height of the mold. Place a second mat and board over the top of the mold. With one hand holding the board Hrmly against the mat and mold, lift and gently Hip over the bottom board and mat with the mold and place back onto the draining rack; the second board and mat will now be on the bottom and the original mat and board will be on top.

8. Let drain for 2 hours, until the curds are reduced in size by about one-third, then ip again in the same manner and let drain overnight at room temperature. The curds will be about 1½ inches high at this point.

9. Salt the top of the cheese, ip it over, salt the second side, and let drain for 2 more hours. The quantity of salt is

hard to pinpoint, but if you imagine salting a steak or tomato well, that is about right. The curds will be about 1 inch high at this point. Remove the mold and spray the cheese lightly (while it is on the draining rack) with the P. candidum solution.

10.   Place the cheese on a clean cheese mat in a ripening box. Cover loosely with the lid and ripen at 50°F to 55°F and 90 percent humidity. High humidity is essential for making this cheese. Flip the cheese daily, removing any whey that may have accumulated in the ripening box. Keep the box loosely covered to maintain the humidity level.

11.   After 2 days, you can lightly spray the cheeses with mold solution again to help ensure proper mold growth, if desired. After about 5 days, the Hrst signs of white fuzzy mold will appear. Remove any undesirable mold with a piece of cheesecloth dipped in a vinegar-salt solution.

12. After 10 to 14 days, the cheeses will be fully coated in white mold. At this point, clean the ripening box, wrap the cheeses in cheese paper, and return them to the ripening box.

13. The cheese will begin to soften within 1 week or so. After a total of 4 weeks from the start of ripening (or 3 weeks if you use Camembert molds), move the wrapped cheeses to the refrigerator and store until they have reached the desired ripeness: rm and mild, or runny and strong.

14. The aging time to desired ripeness will vary depending on the diameter and thickness of the cheese: if a Brie mold was used, count on 4 to 7 weeks total; if 2 Camembert molds, count on 3 to 6 weeks total.

8. American-style brie

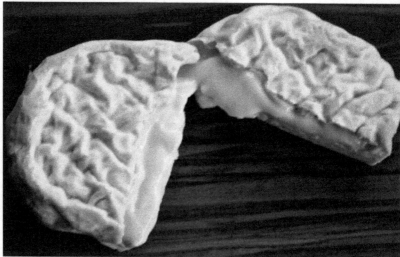

MAKES 2 pounds

- 2 gallons pasteurized whole cow's milk
- ½ cup pasteurized heavy cream
- Pinch of MA 4001 powdered mesophilic starter culture
- 1 teaspoon Thermo B powdered thermophilic starter culture
- 1 teaspoon Penicillium candidum mold powder
- 1 teaspoon Geotrichum candidum 15 mold powder
- 1 teaspoon calcium chloride diluted in ¼ cup cool nonchlorinated water

- 1 teaspoon liquid rennet diluted in ¼ cup cool nonchlorinated water
- Kosher salt (preferably Diamond Crystal brand) or cheese salt

1. Heat the milk and cream in a 10-quart stockpot set in a 102°F water bath over low heat. Bring the milk to 90°F over 10 minutes.

2. Leave the heat on and sprinkle the starter cultures and mold powders over the milk and let rehydrate for 5 minutes. Mix well using a whisk in an up-and-down motion for 20 strokes. Allow the temperature of the milk to rise to 96°F to 98°F. Turn o the heat, cover, and let the milk rest in the water bath for 1½ hours. Add the calcium chloride and gently whisk in, then add the rennet in the same way. Let rest, covered, for 30 minutes, or until the curds give a clean break.

3. Cut the curds into ¾-inch pieces and let sit for 5 minutes. Stir the curds for 10 to 15 minutes, then let them settle for 5 minutes. Ladle o   enough whey to expose the curds.

4. Set a draining rack over a tray, put an 8-inch Brie mold (with a bottom) on it, and put the rack in a ripening box. Gently ladle the curds into the mold and let the curds drain for 1 hour, periodically lifting the mold and pouring the whey out of the tray.

5. After 1 hour, gently Rip the cheese out of the mold into your hand, turn it over, and return it to the mold. This evens out the drainage and smoothes the surface on both sides. Flip the cheese every hour as you continue to drain and discard whey. Gradually there will only be a few

ounces of whey to drain. When there is no more whey, after four or ve ips, put a foil cover or lid on the ripening box, vented in two places, and keep the box at room temperature for 8 hours.

6.   Drain oD the last of the whey and unmold the cheese onto a mat. Salt the top of the cheese, ip it over, and salt the second side. The quantity of salt is hard to pinpoint, but if you imagine salting a steak or tomato well, that is about right. Salting the edges is optional.

7.   The blooming phase of ripening begins now and is best carried out at 52°F to 56°F. Put the lid of the ripening box on askew or cover the middle two-thirds of the pan with aluminum foil, leaving it open at both ends for air circulation. In 3 to 4 days the cheese will bloom, with white mold forming over the surface. Flip the wheel over to bloom the other side. The second bloom will be complete in only 1 or 2 more days.

8.   Using cheese paper, wrap the wheel, taping closed any awkward edges. Move the wheel to a clean tray and ripening box with a closed lid. Place 2 wadded damp paper towels at opposite corners of the box to keep the humidity at about 85 percent. Move this box to your refrigerator (set at about 38°F). Moisten the towels as needed and turn the wheel over once or twice during the ripening time.

9.   The wheel should be ready to serve after 5 to 6 weeks. You can check by cutting out a small ¼-inch wedge. The

cheese should feel soft and begin to ooze out of the rind, and it should taste and smell mild (old Brie will taste very tangy and smell of ammonia).

10. Press a small piece of waxed paper into the cut section before rewrapping. The cheese will keep for 6 to 8 weeks in the refrigerator.

9. Bucheron

MAKES Two 8-ounce logs

- Penicillium candidum mold powder
- 1¾ teaspoons Vne sea salt
- 1 gallon pasteurized goat's milk
- 1 teaspoon Aroma B powdered mesophilic starter culture
- Pinch of Geotrichum candidum 15 mold powder
- 1 teaspoon calcium chloride diluted in ¼ cup cool nonchlorinated water
- 1 teaspoon liquid rennet diluted in ¼ cup cool nonchlorinated water

1. Twelve hours before starting, combine a pinch of P. candidum, ¼ teaspoon of the salt, and 2 cups of cool nonchlorinated water in an atomizer or spray bottle. Store at 50°F to 55°F.

2. In a non-reactive 6-quart stockpot, heat the milk over low heat to 72°F; this should take about 10 minutes. Turn oP the heat.

3. Sprinkle the starter, ⅛ teaspoon of P. candidum mold powder, and the Geotrichum candidum mold powder over the milk and let rehydrate for 5 minutes. Mix well using a whisk in an up-and-down motion for 20 strokes. Add the calcium chloride and gently whisk in for 1 minute, then add the rennet in the same way. Cover and let sit, maintaining 72°F, for 18 hours, or until the curds are a rm mass and whey is oating on top.

4. Place a draining rack over a tray. Steady 2 cylindrical Saint-Maure or bûche molds inside 2 round, straight-sided molds and place on the rack.

5. Gently cut ½-inch-thick slices of curds using a ladle or skimmer and gently ladle the slices into the cylindrical molds to ll. Let drain until more curds can be added to the molds. Do not be tempted to add another mold; the curds will compress as the whey drains out, making room for all of the curds.

6.	When all the curds have been ladled into the molds, cover them with a clean kitchen towel and let the cheeses drain for 24 hours at room temperature. Remove any collected whey a few times while draining, wiping out the tray with a paper towel each time.

7.	After 6 hours, or when the cheeses are firm enough to handle, gently invert the molds onto your palm to ip the cheeses in their molds. Do this a few more times during the 24 hours to aid in uniform formation of the cheeses and development of the bacteria. At the end of 24 hours, the curds will have reduced to about half the height of the molds.

8.	Once the cheeses have stopped draining and the curds have compressed to below the halfway point of the mold, place a mat in a ripening box. Remove the cheeses from the molds and sprinkle ¾ teaspoon of the salt over the entire surface of each cheese.

9.	Set the cheeses at least 1 inch apart on the mat in the ripening box and allow 10 minutes for the salt to dissolve, then mist lightly with the P. candidum solution. Wipe any moisture from the walls of the box. Cover the box loosely with the lid and let it stand at room temperature for 24 hours.

10.	Drain any whey and wipe out any moisture from the box, then ripen the cheese at 50°F to 55°F and 90 percent humidity for 2 weeks. For the Lrst few days, adjust the lid to be slightly open for a portion of each day to maintain the desired humidity level.

11. Too much humidity will create an undesirably wet surface. The surface of the cheese should appear moist but not wet. Each day, wipe out any moisture that may have accumulated in the ripening box. Throughout the ripening period, turn the cheeses one-quarter turn daily to maintain their log shape.

12. After 2 days, very lightly mist with the mold solution. After about 5 days, the rst signs of white fuzzy mold will appear. After 10 to 14 days, the cheeses will be fully coated in white mold. Remove any undesirable mold using a piece of cheesecloth dipped in a vinegar-salt solution.

13. Clean and dry the ripening box, wrap the cheeses in cheese paper, and return them to the ripening box. The cheeses will begin to soften within 1 week or so.

14. After a total of 4 weeks from the start of ripening, wrap in plastic wrap and store in the refrigerator. It is best to consume this cheese when it has reached the desired ripeness, between 4 weeks and 5 weeks.

10. Camembert

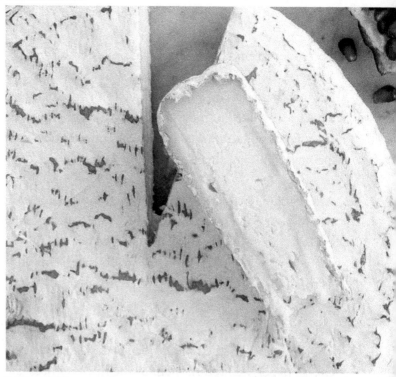

MAKES 1 pound

- 3 quarts pasteurized whole cow's milk
- 1 teaspoon MM 100 powdered mesophilic starter culture
- ⅛ teaspoon Penicillium candidum mold powder
- 1 teaspoon calcium chloride diluted in ¼ cup cool nonchlorinated water
- 1 teaspoon liquid rennet diluted in ¼ cup cool nonchlorinated water
- 5 tablespoons kosher salt (preferably Diamond Crystal brand) or cheese salt

1. In a nonreactive 6-quart stockpot, heat the milk over low heat to 90°F; this should take about 20 minutes. Turn off the heat.

2. Sprinkle the starter and mold powder over the milk and let rehydrate for 5 minutes. Mix well using a whisk in an up-and-down motion.

3. Cover and maintain 90°F, letting the milk ripen for 1½ hours. Add the calcium chloride and gently whisk in, then add the rennet in the same way. Cover and let sit, maintaining 90°F, until the curds give a clean break.

4. Cut the curds into ¼- to ½-inch pieces and let sit for 5 minutes. Gently stir with a rubber spatula to prevent the curd from matting together, then ladle o one-third of the whey. Add the salt and gently stir to incorporate.

5. Ladle the curds into an 4-inch Camembert mold set on a draining rack over a tray. Let drain at room temperature until the cheese is rm enough to ip, about 2 hours. Flip the cheese every hour for 5 hours or until it stops draining.

11. Coulommiers

MAKES Four 5-ounce cheeses

- Penicillium candidum mold powder
- 3½ teaspoons kosher or Vne Nake sea salt
- 2 gallons pasteurized whole cow's milk
- 1 teaspoon MA 4001 powdered mesophilic starter culture
- 1 teaspoon calcium chloride diluted in ¼ cup cool nonchlorinated water
- 1 teaspoon liquid rennet diluted in ¼ cup cool nonchlorinated water

1. Twelve hours before starting, combine a pinch of of P. candidum, ½ teaspoon of salt, and 1 quart of

nonchlorinated water in an atomizer or spray bottle. Store at 50°F to 55°F.

2. In a nonreactive 10-quart stockpot, heat the milk over low heat to 90°F; this should take about 20 minutes. Turn oP the heat.

3. Sprinkle the starter and ⅛ teaspoon of P. candidum mold powder over the milk and let rehydrate for 5 minutes. Mix well using a whisk in an up-and-down motion. Add the calcium chloride and gently whisk in, then add the rennet in the same way. Cover and let sit, maintaining 90°F for 1½ hours, or until the curds give a clean break.

4. Cut the curds into ½-inch thick slices and let sit for 5 minutes to rm up the curds. Using a rubber spatula, gently stir around the edges of the pot for 5 minutes to shrink the curds slightly and keep them from matting.

5. Set a draining rack over a tray, put a cutting board on the rack and a cheese mat on the board, and, nally, place four 4-inch Camembert molds on the mat. Using a skimmer, gently ladle the slices of curds into the molds. Fill the molds to the top, then continue to add slices as the curds drain.

6. When all the curds have been transferred to the molds, cover the molds with a clean kitchen towel and let drain at room temperature for 5 to 6 hours, or until the curds

have reduced to almost half the height of the molds. Discard the whey periodically.

7. Place a second mat and cutting board over the top of the molds. With one hand holding the top board Wrmly against the mat and molds, lift and gently ip over the bottom board and mat with the molds and place back onto the draining rack; the second board and mat will now be on the bottom and the original mat and board will be on top.

8.   Let drain for 6 hours, until the curds are about 1½ to 2 inches high, then Gip again and let drain for another 3 hours. Stop ipping once the cheeses stop draining; they should be well drained and Orm to the touch.

9.   Remove the molds and sprinkle about 1½ teaspoons salt over the tops and sides of the cheeses. Leave for 10 minutes, allowing the salt to dissolve. Place the cheeses salt side down on a clean cheese mat in a ripening box and salt the other sides, again using about 1½ teaspoons. Cover the box with the lid slightly open for a little air circulation and ripen the cheeses at 50°F to 55°F and 90 percent humidity. High humidity is essential for making this cheese.

10. Flip the cheeses daily, removing any whey and any moisture that may have accumulated in the ripening box, as moisture will inhibit the proper white mold development. Once moisture no longer accumulates in the box, cover the box tightly.

11. After 2 days, spray lightly with the mold solution. After about 5 days, the rst signs of white fuzzy mold will appear. After 10 to 14 days, the cheeses will be fully coated in white mold. Remove any undesirable mold using a piece of cheesecloth dipped in a vinegar-salt solution.

12. Clean the ripening box, wrap the cheeses in cheese paper, and return them to the ripening box. The cheese will begin to soften within 1 week or so. It is ready to eat when the center feels soft to the touch; this can be 1 to 2 weeks or slightly longer. Store in the refrigerator until they reach the desired ripeness.

12. Craggy cloaked cabra

MAKES Ten 3-ounce cheeses

- Penicillium candidum mold powder
- 4¼ teaspoons Vne sea salt
- 1 gallon pasteurized goat's milk
- 1 teaspoon Aroma B powdered mesophilic starter culture
  Pinch of Geotrichum candidum 15 mold powder
- 1 teaspoon calcium chloride diluted in ¼ cup cool
  nonchlorinated water
- 1 teaspoon liquid rennet diluted in ¼ cup cool
  nonchlorinated water
- 2 tablespoons vegetable ash

1. Twelve hours before starting, combine a pinch of P. candidum, ¼ teaspoon of the salt, and 2 cups of cool nonchlorinated water in an atomizer or spray bottle. Store at 50°F to 55°F.

2. In a nonreactive 6-quart stockpot, heat the milk over low heat to 72°F; this should take about 10 minutes. Turn off the heat.

3. Sprinkle the starter, ⅛ teaspoon of P. candidum, and the Geotrichum candidum mold powder over the milk and let rehydrate for 5 minutes. Mix well using a whisk in an up-and-down motion for 20 strokes. Cover and maintain 72°F, letting the milk ripen for 30 minutes. Add the calcium chloride and gently whisk in for 1 minute, then add the rennet in the same way. Cover and let sit, maintaining 72°F for 8 to 10 hours, or until the curds give a clean break.

4. Cut the curds into ½-inch pieces and let sit for 5 minutes. Gently stir for 10 minutes with a rubber spatula, then ladle the curds into a colander lined with damp butter muslin and let drain for 30 minutes. Sprinkle in 1 tablespoon of the salt and gently toss with your hands to incorporate, then make a draining sack from the muslin and let drain for 4 hours, or until the whey stops dripping.

5. Using a scale, portion the drained curds into 10 pieces; each should weigh approximately 3½ ounces. Lightly shape and roll into balls, then place the cheeses at least 1 inch apart on a mat set in a ripening box. Cover

the box loosely with the lid and let stand at room temperature for 8 hours.

6.   Drain the whey and wipe out any moisture from the box, then ripen the cheese at 50°F to 55°F and 85 percent humidity for 2 days. Adjust the lid to be slightly open for a portion of each day to maintain the desired humidity level. The surface of the cheese should appear moist but not wet.

7.   In a small bowl or jar, combine the vegetable ash with the remaining 1 teaspoon of salt. Wearing disposable gloves, use a Vne-mesh strainer to dust the cheeses with the vegetable ash, coating them completely. Gently pat the ash onto the surface of the cheeses. Place the dusted cheeses on a clean cheese mat in a dry ripening box. Ripen at 50°F to 55°F and 85 percent humidity, turning the cheeses daily to maintain the round shape.

8.   Two days after you have ashed the cheeses, very lightly mist them with the mold solution. Secure the lid on the ripening box. After about 5 days, the rst signs of white fuzzy mold will appear through the ash. After 10 to 14 days, the cheeses will be fully coated in white mold. The wrinkled surface will also begin to develop within 10 days.

9.   At 2 weeks, clean and dry the ripening box, wrap the cheeses in cheese paper, and return them to the ripening box. The cheeses will begin to soften within 1 week or so. After a total of 3 weeks from the start of ripening, store

them in the refrigerator. It is best to consume these cheeses when they have reached the desired ripeness, about 3 to 4 weeks from the start of ripening.

13. Crottin

MAKES Four 3½-ounce cheeses

- 1 gallon pasteurized goat's milk

- 1 teaspoon Meso I or Aroma B powdered mesophilic starter culture Pinch of Penicillium candidum mold powder
- Pinch of Geotrichum candidum 15 mold powder
- 1 teaspoon calcium chloride diluted in ¼ cup cool nonchlorinated water
- 1 teaspoon liquid rennet diluted in ¼ cup cool nonchlorinated water
- 1 tablespoon Hne sea salt

1. Let the milk sit at room temperature for 1 hour. In a nonreactive 6-quart stockpot, heat the milk over low heat to 72°F; this should take about 10 minutes. Turn o the heat.

2. Sprinkle the starter and the mold powders over the milk and let rehydrate for 5 minutes. Mix well using a whisk in an up-and-down motion. Add the calcium chloride and gently whisk in for 1 minute, then add the rennet in the same way. Cover and maintain 72°F, letting the milk ripen for 18 hours, or until the curds form a solid mass.

3. Place 4 crottin molds on a draining rack set over a tray. Gently cut ½-inch-thick slices of the curds using a ladle or skimmer and gently ladle the slices of curds into the molds to ll. Drain until more curds can be added to the molds. Do not be tempted to add another mold; the curds will compress as the whey drains out, making room for all of the curds.

4. When all of the curds have been ladled into the molds, cover them with a clean kitchen towel and let the

cheeses drain at room temperature. Remove any collected whey a few times while draining, wiping out the tray with a paper towel each time.

5. After 12 hours, or when the cheeses are Wrm enough to handle, gently invert the molds onto your palm to ip the cheeses in their molds. Do this three more times during the next 36 hours to aid in uniform formation of the cheeses and development of the bacteria. After 48 hours, the curds will have reduced to about half the height of the mold.

6.   Once the cheeses have stopped draining and the curds have compressed to below the halfway point of the mold, place a mat in a ripening box. Remove the cheeses from the molds and sprinkle the salt over the tops and bottoms of the cheeses. Set them at least 1 inch apart on the mat in the ripening box and allow 10 minutes for the salt to dissolve. Wipe any moisture from the walls of the box.

7.   Cover the box loosely with the lid and let it stand at room temperature for 8 hours. Drain any whey and wipe out any moisture from the box, then ripen the cheeses at 50°F

8. to 55°F and 90 percent humidity, Hipping the cheeses daily. For the rst few days, adjust the lid to be slightly open for a portion of each day to maintain the desired humidity level. Too much humidity will create an

undesirably wet surface. The surface of the cheeses should appear moist but not wet.

9. After about 5 days, the rst signs of white fuzzy mold will appear. After 10 to 14 days, the cheeses will be fully coated in white mold. Clean and dry the ripening box, wrap the cheeses in cheese paper, and return them to the ripening box.

10. The cheeses will begin to soften within 1 week or so. After a total of 3 weeks from the start of ripening, wrap the cheeses in fresh cheese paper and store in the refrigerator. It is best to consume these cheeses when they have reached the desired ripeness, between 3 and 4 weeks from the beginning of ripening.

14. Fromage à l'Huile

MAKES Four 6-ounce crottin disks

- 2 gallons pasteurized goat's milk
- 1 teaspoon MM 100 or MA 011 powdered mesophilic starter culture Pinch of Choozit CUM yeast
- Pinch of Penicillium candidum mold powder Pinch of Geotrichum candidum 17 mold powder
- ¼ teaspoon calcium chloride diluted in ½ cup cool nonchlorinated water ¼ teaspoon liquid rennet diluted in ½ cup cool nonchlorinated water
- 2 teaspoons kosher salt (preferably Diamond Crystal brand) or cheese salt

1. In a nonreactive 10-quart stockpot, heat the milk over medium heat to 75°F; this should take about 12 minutes. Turn offthe heat.

2. Sprinkle the starter, yeast, and mold powders over the milk and let rehydrate for 5 minutes. Mix well using a whisk in an up-and-down motion.

3. Cover and maintain 75°F, letting the milk ripen for 25 minutes. Gently whisk in the calcium chloride for 1 minute, and then add the rennet in the same way.

4. Cover and let sit, maintaining 75°F for 15 to 20 hours, until the pH of the whey is below 4.6 but not lower than 4.4. At this point, the curds will have separated from the sides of the vat and there will be cracks in the body of the curds and a ½-inch layer of whey on top of the curds.

5. Set a draining rack over a tray and place 4 crottin molds on the rack. The curd can be ladled in large scoops and drained in damp cheesecloth for 10 to 15 hours and then packed into the crottin molds or gently ladled in small scoops directly into the molds. Either way, once the curds are in the molds, let them drain for 15 to 36 hours at room temperature.

6. Sprinkle ¼ teaspoon of kosher salt over the top of each cheese in its mold. After about 10 hours of draining, the curds will be rm and hold their shape.

7. After 12 hours total draining time, unmold the cheeses, Pip them, and return them to the molds and the rack to drain further. Sprinkle another ¼ teaspoon of salt over the top of each cheese in its mold.

8.   Unmold the cheeses and set them on a cheese mat to air-dry at 60°F to 65°F. Flip the cheeses the next day, then let them sit until there is visible mold growth on the surface; this should take 3 to 5 days.

9. When there is growth, ip the cheeses over and move them to a more humid and colder place, in a ripening box at 45°F to 48°F and 90 percent humidity. Flip the cheeses daily until they are completely covered with white mold; this should happen within 10 days.

10. After a total of 2 weeks from the start of ripening, wrap the cheeses in cheese paper and store in the refrigerator.

11. It is best to consume these cheeses when they have reached the desired ripeness, between 2 and 3 weeks from the beginning of ripening, or longer for a stronger avor.

15. Mushroom-infused camembert

MAKES Two 8-ounce cheeses

- Penicillium candidum mold powder
- 4½ teaspoons kosher salt (preferably Diamond Crystal brand), cheese salt, or Lne Pake sea salt
- 1 ounce dried sliced shiitake mushrooms 1 gallon pasteurized whole cow's milk
- ¼ teaspoon MM 100 powdered mesophilic starter culture Pinch of Geotrichum candidum 15 mold powder
- ¼ teaspoon calcium chloride diluted in ¼ cup cool nonchlorinated water ¼ teaspoon liquid rennet diluted in ¼ cup cool nonchlorinated water
1. Twelve hours before starting, combine a pinch of P. candidum, ½ teaspoon of salt, and 1 quart of cool nonchlorinated water in an atomizer or spray bottle. Store at 50°F to 55°F.

2.   In a nonreactive 6-quart stockpot, stir the mushrooms into the milk, then heat over low heat to 110°F to 112°F. Turn o the heat and maintain temperature for 55 minutes. Strain the milk through a ne-mesh strainer, pressing down on the mushrooms to squeeze out any liquid. Discard the mushrooms.

3.   Cool the milk to 90°F, then sprinkle the starter, ⅛ teaspoon of P. candidum mold powder, and the Geotrichum candidum mold powder over the milk and let rehydrate for 5 minutes. Mix well using a whisk in an up-and-down motion. Add the calcium chloride and gently whisk in, then add the rennet in the same way. Cover and let sit, maintaining a temperature of 85°F for 1½ hours, or until the curds give a clean break.

4.   4. Cut the curds into ½-inch pieces and let sit for 5 minutes to rm up. Using a rubber spatula, gently stir around the edges of the pot for 5 minutes to shrink the curds and keep them from matting. Let the curds rest for 5 minutes; they will sink to the bottom.

5.   Set a draining rack over a tray, put a cutting board on the rack and a cheese mat on the board, and, nally, place the two 4-inch Camembert molds on the mat. Ladle o some of the whey and, using a skimmer, gently ladle the curds into the molds. Let drain for 2 hours, until the curds have reduced to about half the height of the molds.

6.   Place a second mat and cutting board over the top of the molds. With one hand holding the top board rmly

against the mat and molds, lift and gently Gip the molds over and set them back onto the draining rack.

7. Let drain for 2 hours, then ip again. At this point the curds should be 1½ to 2 inches high. Cover and let drain at room temperature for 8 hours or overnight. Flip the cheeses again and let drain for 2 more hours.

8. Remove the molds and sprinkle about 2 teaspoons of salt over the top and sides of the cheeses. Leave for 10 minutes, allowing the salt to dissolve. At this point, spray lightly with the mold solution. Place the cheeses salt side down on a clean mat in a ripening box and salt the other side, using the remaining 2 teaspoons of salt.

9. Cover the box with the lid slightly open for a little air circulation and ripen the cheeses at 50°F to 55°F and 90 percent humidity. High humidity is essential for making this cheese. Flip the cheeses daily, removing any whey and any moisture that may have accumulated in the ripening box. Keep covered to maintain the humidity level.

10. After about 5 days, the rst signs of white fuzzy mold will appear. Continue to ip the cheeses daily.

11. After 10 to 14 days, the cheeses will be fully coated in white mold. Wrap them loosely in cheese paper and return them to the ripening box at 50°F to 55°F and 85 percent humidity. The cheeses will begin to soften within 1 week or so.

12. After a total of 4 weeks from the start of ripening, move the cheeses to the refrigerator until they reach the desired ripeness, up to 6 weeks from the start of ripening.

16. Bloomy robiola

MAKES 2 pounds

- Robiola
- 1 gallon pasteurized whole cow's milk
- 1 gallon pasteurized goat's milk
- 1 teaspoon MM 100 powdered mesophilic starter culture
- 1 teaspoon Geotrichum candidum 15 mold powder
- 1 teaspoon calcium chloride diluted in ¼ cup cool nonchlorinated water 4 drops rennet diluted in ¼ cup nonchlorinated water
- Kosher salt (preferably Diamond Crystal brand)

1. In a nonreactive 10-quart stockpot, heat the milks over low heat to 95°F; this should take about 25 minutes. Turn off the heat.

2. Sprinkle the starter and mold powder over the milks and let rehydrate for 5 minutes. Mix well using a whisk in an up-and-down motion. Add the calcium chloride and gently whisk in, and then add the rennet in the same way. Cover and let sit, maintaining 95°F for up to 18 hours, or until the curds give a clean break.

3. Set a draining rack over a tray, followed by a cheese mat. Place 2 Camembert molds on the mat. Using a skimmer, gently ladle the curds into the molds. Let drain at room temperature for 8 to 10 hours, or until the curds have compressed to 1½ to 2 inches.

4. Sprinkle ¼ teaspoon of kosher salt over the top of each cheese in its mold. After 10 to 12 hours of draining, the curds will be rm and hold their shape. Unmold the cheeses, ip them, and return them to the rack to drain further. Sprinkle another ¼ teaspoon of salt over the top of each cheese.

5. Let the cheeses drain for 2 hours, then place the cheeses on a clean cheese mat in a ripening box. Cover the box with its lid and let ripen at 77°F and 92 to 95 percent humidity. Every 8 hours, loosen the lid to allow air to circulate.

6. After 30 to 48 hours (depending on when the whey stops draining), lower the temperature to 55°F and keep the humidity at 92 to 95 percent.

7.   After about 5 days, the signs of a creamy white surface will appear. Continue to Pip the cheeses daily and remove any excess moisture from the box. After 7 to 10 days, the cheeses will have a rosy surface hue. After 3 to 4 weeks some blue mold may have formed on the surface.

8. At this point the cheese will be very ripe, and barely contained by its thin rind. You may use the cheeses now, wrap and store them in the refrigerator, or continue aging for up to 3 months.

17. Saint-marcellin

MAKES Four 3-ounce rounds

- 3 quarts pasteurized whole cow's milk
- 1 teaspoon Meso II powdered mesophilic starter culture
  Pinch of Penicillium candidum mold powder
- Pinch of Geotrichum candidum 15 mold powder
- ¼ teaspoon calcium chloride diluted in ¼ cup cool
  nonchlorinated water 6 drops liquid rennet diluted in ¼
  cup cool nonchlorinated water
- 3 teaspoons kosher salt (preferably Diamond Crystal
  brand) or cheese salt

1. In a nonreactive 4-quart stockpot, heat the milk over low
   heat to 75°F; this should take about 12 minutes. Turn off
   the heat.

2.   Sprinkle the starter and mold powders over the milk and let rehydrate for 5 minutes. Mix well using a whisk in an up-and-down motion. Add the calcium chloride and gently whisk in, then add the rennet in the same way. Cover and let sit, maintaining 72°F to 75°F for 12 hours.

3.   Cut the curds into ½-inch slices using a ladle or skimmer. Using a rubber spatula, gently stir around the edges of the pot, then let the curds stand for 5 minutes.

4.   Set a draining rack over a tray, then place 4 Saint-Marcellin molds on the rack. Ladle the curds into a colander or strainer lined with damp butter muslin and let drain for 15 minutes. Ladle the curds into the molds up to their tops, then let drain until more curds can be added to the molds.

5.   Do not be tempted to add another mold; the curds will compress as the whey drains out. The process will take about 30 minutes. Drain the curds at room temperature. After 6 hours, ip the cheeses in the molds and sprinkle the tops with 1½ teaspoons of the salt. Let drain for another 6 hours, then Wip the cheeses in the molds again and sprinkle the tops with the remaining 1½ teaspoons of salt and drain for another 6 hours.

6.   Unmold the cheeses and place them on a cheese mat in a ripening box. Cover the box loosely and let the cheeses drain at room temperature for 48 hours, ipping the cheeses daily and removing any whey that has accumulated.

7.   Ripen at 55°F and 90 percent humidity for 14 days, or until a white fuzzy mold has developed to cover the cheese, Yipping the cheeses daily and continuing to remove the whey. The cheeses are ready to eat at this point, or they can be aged further.

8.   Place each disk in a shallow clay crock and cover with plastic wrap or the crock's lid. If crocks are not used, wrap the cheeses in cheese paper or plastic wrap and store in the refrigerator for up to 6 weeks.

18. Valençay

MAKES Four 3- to 4-ounce pyramid-shaped cheeses

- 1 gallon pasteurized goat's milk
- 1 teaspoon Meso I or Aroma B powdered mesophilic starter culture ⅛ teaspoon Penicillium candidum mold powder
- Pinch of Geotrichum candidum 15 mold powder
- 1 teaspoon calcium chloride diluted in ¼ cup cool nonchlorinated water
- 1 teaspoon liquid rennet diluted in ¼ cup cool nonchlorinated water
- 1 cup vegetable ash powder
- 2 teaspoon sea salt

1. In a nonreactive 6-quart stockpot, heat the milk over low heat to 72°F; this should take about 10 minutes. Turn off the heat.

2. Sprinkle the starter and mold powders over the surface of the milk and let rehydrate for 5 minutes. Mix well using a whisk in an up-and-down motion. Add the calcium chloride and gently whisk in for 1 minute, then add the rennet in the same way. Cover and let sit, maintaining 72°F for 12 hours or until the curds give a clean break.

3. Cut the curds into ½-inch slices using a ladle or skimmer. Using a rubber spatula, gently stir around the edges of the pot for 5 minutes, then let the curds stand for 5 minutes.

4. Set a draining rack on a tray, then place 4 truncated pyramid molds on the rack. Ladle the slices of curds into the molds to ll, then let drain until more curds can be added to the molds. Do not be tempted to add another mold; the curds will compress as the whey drains out.

5. Cover with a dish towel and let the cheeses drain for 48 hours at room temperature, removing any whey a few times while draining and removing any collected whey with a paper towel each time you drain it. Flip the molds after 12 hours or when the cheeses are rm enough to handle, then Xip a few more times during the next 36 hours. At the end of 48 hours, the curds will have reduced to about half the height of the mold.

6.   Remove the molds and combine the vegetable ash with the salt in a small bowl. Wearing disposable gloves, use a One-mesh strainer to dust the cheeses with vegetable ash, lightly coating each completely. Gently pat the ash onto the surface of the cheeses.

7.   Place the cheeses at least 1 inch apart on a clean cheese mat in a ripening box. Cover loosely with the lid and let stand at room temperature for 24 hours. Wipe out any moisture from the box, then ripen at 50°F to 55°F and 90 percent humidity for 3 weeks.

8.   For the rst few days, adjust the lid to be slightly open for a portion of each day to maintain the desired humidity level. The surface of the cheeses should appear moist but not wet.

9.   Continue to ip the cheeses daily. After about 5 days, the Grst signs of white fuzzy mold will appear through the ash. After 10 to 14 days the cheeses will be fully coated in white mold. As the cheese continues to age, the surface will turn a very light gray.

10.   Wrap the cheeses in cheese paper and return them to the ripening box; they will begin to soften within 1 week or so. After a total of 4 weeks from the start of ripening, wrap the cheeses in fresh cheese paper and store them in the refrigerator. It is best to consume this cheese when it has reached the desired ripeness, within 4 to 6 weeks from the start of ripening.

WASHED-RIND AND SMEARED-RIND CHEESES

19. Ale-washed coriander trappist cheese

MAKES 1 pound

- 1 gallon pasteurized whole cow's milk
- 1½ teaspoons coriander seeds, crushed
- 1½ teaspoons granulated orange peel
- 1 teaspoon Meso II powdered mesophilic starter culture
- 1 teaspoon calcium chloride diluted in ¼ cup cool nonchlorinated water
- 1 teaspoon liquid rennet diluted in ¼ cup cool nonchlorinated water
- Kosher salt (preferably Diamond Crystal brand)
- One 12-ounce bottle Belgian ale at room temperature, plus 16 to 24 ounces more for washing

1. In a nonreactive 2-quart saucepan, heat 1 quart of the milk over low heat to 90°F; this should take about 20 minutes. Stir in 1 teaspoon of the coriander and 1 teaspoon of the orange peel, then slowly raise the temperature to 110°F over the course of 10 minutes. Turn o the heat, cover, and let steep for 45 minutes, or until the temperature drops back down to 90°F.

2. Place the remaining 3 quarts of milk in a nonreactive 6-quart stockpot. Pour the steeped milk through a Nne-mesh strainer into the larger pot of milk and whisk to combine. Discard the coriander and orange. Bring the milk to 90°F over low heat; this should take 5 minutes. Turn oP the heat.

3. Sprinkle the starter over the milk and let it rehydrate for 5 minutes. Mix well using a whisk in an up-and-down motion. Cover and maintain 90°F, allowing the milk to ripen for few minutes. Add the calcium chloride and gently whisk in for 1 minute, then add the rennet in the same way. Cover and let sit, maintaining 90°F for 1 hour, or until the curds give a clean break.

4. Still maintaining 90°F, cut the curds into ½-inch pieces and let sit for 10 minutes. Gently stir the curds for 15 minutes to expel more whey, then let settle for another 10 minutes. The curds will shrink to the size of small beans. Meanwhile, heat 2 quarts of water to 175°F. Ladle o enough whey to expose the curds. Add enough hot water to bring the temperature to 93°F.

5. Stir for 10 minutes. Repeat the process of removing whey and adding hot water, this time bringing the temperature

to 100°F. Stir for 15 minutes, then let the curds settle for 10 minutes. Cover and let rest for 45 minutes, maintaining 100°F. The curds will mat and form a slab.

6.   Drain oD enough whey to expose the slab of curds. Transfer the slab to a Vat-bottomed colander, place it over the pot, and let drain for 5 minutes. Transfer the slab to a cutting board and cut into ⅜-inch-thick slices. Place in a bowl and gently toss with 2 teaspoons of the salt.

7.   Line a 5-inch tomme mold with damp cheesecloth and set it on a draining rack. Tightly pack half of the curds in the mold, cover with the cloth tails and the follower, and press at 5 pounds for 10 minutes, just to compact the curds slightly. Peel back the cloth and sprinkle on the remaining ½ teaspoon of coriander and ½ teaspoon of orange peel, then pack in the rest of the milled curds.

8. Cover with the cloth tails and the follower and press at 8 pounds for 6 hours at room temperature. Remove the cheese from the mold, unwrap, ip, and redress, then press again at 8 pounds for 8 hours to thoroughly compress the curds.

9.   Pour the bottle of ale into a lidded nonreactive container large enough to hold both ale and cheese. Remove the cheese from the mold and cheesecloth and place in the ale. Soak the cheese, covered, for 8 hours at 55°F, tipping once.

10.   Remove the cheese from the ale and pat dry. Reserve and refrigerate the ale and place the cheese on a cheese mat. Air-dry at room temperature for 12 hours. Return the cheese to the ale and soak for another 12 hours at 55°F. Remove, pat dry, and air-dry at room temperature for 12 hours, or until the surface is dry to the touch. Discard the ale.

11.   Prepare a brine-ale wash: boil ½ cup of water and let it cool, and combine with ½ cup of ale, then dissolve 1 teaspoon of salt in the liquid. Store in the refrigerator.

12.   Place the cheese on a mat in a ripening box and ripen at 50°F and 90 percent humidity for 4 to 6 weeks. Flip the cheese daily for the Orst 2 weeks, then twice weekly thereafter.

13. After each tip, pour a little brine-ale wash into a small dish, dip a small piece of cheesecloth in it, and use it to wipe the surface of the cheese. Discard any unused brine-ale wash after 1 week and make a fresh batch. Also wipe away any moisture from the bottom, sides, and lid of the ripening box each time you Wip the cheese.

14.   Wrap the cheese in cheese paper and store refrigerated for up to 1 month. If you vacuum-seal the cheese, remove it from the package and pat it dry before consuming it.

20. Cabra al vino

MAKES 1½ pounds

- 2 gallons pasteurized goat's milk

- ¼ teaspoon Meso II powdered mesophilic starter culture
- 1 teaspoon calcium chloride diluted in ¼ cup cool nonchlorinated water
- ¾ teaspoon liquid rennet diluted in ¼ cup cool nonchlorinated water
- Kosher salt (preferably Diamond Crystal brand)
- One 750 ml bottle red wine, chilled to 55°F

1. In a nonreactive 10-quart stockpot, heat the milk over low heat to 90°F; this should take about 20 minutes. Turn oP the heat.

2. Sprinkle the starter over the milk and let it rehydrate for 5 minutes. Mix well using a whisk in an up-and-down motion. Cover and maintain 90°F, letting the milk ripen for 30 minutes. Add the calcium chloride and gently whisk in for 1 minute, then add the rennet in the same way. Cover and let sit, maintaining 90°F for 1 hour, or until the curds give a clean break.

3. Still maintaining 90°F, cut the curds into ¾-inch pieces and let sit for 5 minutes. Gently stir the curds for 20 minutes, then let settle.

4. Meanwhile, heat 2 quarts of water to 175°F. Ladle o enough whey to expose the curds. Add enough hot water to bring the temperature to 93°F. Stir for 5 minutes. Repeat the process of removing whey and adding hot water, this time bringing the temperature to 102°F. Stir for 15 minutes, and then let the curds settle for 10 minutes.

5. Cover and let rest for minutes, maintaining 102°F. The curds will mat slightly and form a slab.

6. Drain over enough whey to expose the slab of curds. Using a mesh strainer or ladle, gently turn the curds over every 5 minutes for 15 minutes. Place the slab in a bowl

and, using your hands, break it into ½-inch pieces and gently toss with 2 teaspoon of the salt.

7.   Line an 8-inch tomme mold with damp butter muslin and set it on a draining rack. Fill the mold with the milled curds, cover with the tails of the cloth and the follower, and press at 5 pounds for 8 hours at room temperature. Remove the cheese from the mold, unwrap, ip, and redress, then press again at 5 pounds for 8 hours at room temperature.

8.   Pour the wine into a lidded nonreactive container large enough to hold both wine and cheese. Remove the cheese from the mold and cloth and place it in the wine. Soak the cheese, covered, for 12 hours at 55°F, Uipping once.

9.   Remove the cheese from the wine and pat dry. Reserve and refrigerate the wine and place the cheese on a cheese mat. Air-dry at room temperature for 12 hours. Return the cheese to the wine and soak for another 12 hours at 55°F. Remove, pat dry, and air-dry at room temperature for 12 hours, or until the surface is dry to the touch. Discard the wine.

10.   Place the cheese on a mat in a ripening box and ripen at 50°F and 85 percent humidity for 6 weeks. Flip the cheese daily for the rst 2 weeks, then twice weekly thereafter. After each Fip, wipe the surface with a small piece of cheesecloth dipped in a small amount of brine

wash: boil ½ cup of water and let it cool, then add 1 teaspoon of salt and stir to dissolve.

11. Store in the refrigerator. The brine wash will control unwanted mold growth. Discard any unused brine wash after 1 week and make a fresh batch. Also wipe away any moisture from the bottom, sides, and lid of the ripening box each time you Oip the cheese.

12.   After 2 weeks of ripening, you may wax coat the cheese and refrigerate for the duration of the aging time: up to 6 weeks. If you don't want to wax coat, simply keep the cheese in the ripening box for 6 weeks as speciEed in step 9. After 3½ weeks or so, the cheese will have a musty, winery-meets-cheese-shop aroma.

21. Desert sunset pavé

MAKES Two 10-ounce cheeses or one 1½-pound cheese

- 2 gallons pasteurized whole cow's milk
- 1 teaspoon MA 4001 powdered mesophilic starter culture
- ⅛ teaspoon Penicillium candidum mold powder
- Pinch of Geotrichum candidum 15 mold powder
- 1 teaspoon calcium chloride diluted in ¼ cup cool nonchlorinated water
- 1 teaspoon liquid rennet diluted in ¼ cup cool nonchlorinated water
- Kosher salt (preferably Diamond Crystal brand) for brining and washing
- Liquid annatto for brining and washing

1. In a nonreactive 10-quart stockpot, heat the milk over low heat to 90°F; this should take 20 minutes. Turn off the heat.

2. Sprinkle the starter and mold powders over the milk and let rehydrate for 5 minutes. Mix well using a whisk in an up-and-down motion. Cover and maintain 90°F, allowing the milk to ripen for 1 hour. Add the calcium chloride and gently whisk in, then add the rennet in the same way. Cover and let sit, maintaining 90°F for 30 minutes, or until the curds give a clean break.

3. Still maintaining 90°F, cut the curds into ¾-inch pieces and let sit for 5 minutes to rm up. Gently stir the curds for 30 minutes, removing 2 cups of whey every 10 minutes. Then let the curds settle for 10 minutes.

4. Line one 7-inch square Taleggio mold or two 4-inch square cheese molds with damp butter muslin. Place the molds on a draining rack over a tray and gently ladle the curds into the molds, pressing them into the corners with your hand. Cover the curds with the tails of cloth and cover the entire setup with a kitchen towel. Let drain for 6 hours in a warm spot in the kitchen. Remove the cheese from the mold, unwrap, Wip, and redress, then let drain for 6 more hours.

5. Two hours before the end of the draining time, make a soaking brine by combining 2½ cups of cool nonchlorinated water, ½ cup of salt, and 8 drops of annatto in a lidded nonreactive container large enough to hold the brine and cheese.

6. Stir to dissolve the salt completely, then cool to 50°F to 55°F. Remove the cheese from the mold and cloth and place it in the brine. Soak the cheese, covered, at 50°F to 55°F for 8 hours, ipping at least once.

7. Remove the cheese from the brine and pat dry. Air-dry at room temperature on a cheese mat or rack for 24 hours, or until the surface is dry to the touch.

8. Place the cheese on a mat in a ripening box and ripen at 50°F and 85 percent humidity, tipping every other day. At least 2 hours before you Dip the cheese the rest time, make a brine wash by combining 1½ teaspoons of salt, 3 drops of annatto, and 1 cup of cool nonchlorinated water in a sterilized glass jar; shake well to dissolve the salt, then chill to 50°F to 55°F.

9. After each Wip, pour a little brine wash into a small dish, dip a small piece of cheesecloth in it, wring it out, and use it to wipe the surface of the cheese.

10. Discard any unused brine wash after 1 week and make a fresh batch. Also wipe away any moisture from the bottom, sides, and lid of the ripening box each time you Oip the cheese. 8.

11. The rind will become crusty and rm, and in 10 to 14 days an orange color will develop; this will deepen as the cheeses age. After 4 weeks, the rind should be slightly moist and the center of the cheese should feel soft; at this point, it's ready to eat. Consume within 2 weeks.

22. Washed-rind teleme-style

MAKES 2 pounds

- 2 gallons pasteurized whole cow's milk
- 1 teaspoon MA 4001 powdered mesophilic starter culture
- 1 teaspoon calcium chloride diluted in ¼ cup cool nonchlorinated water
- 1 teaspoon liquid rennet diluted in ¼ cup cool nonchlorinated water
- 2 tablespoons kosher salt (preferably Diamond Crystal brand) or cheese salt

1. In a nonreactive 10-quart stockpot, heat the milk over low heat to 86°F; this should take 15 minutes. Turn off the heat.

2. Sprinkle the starter over the milk and let it rehydrate for 5 minutes. Mix well using a whisk in an up-and-down motion. Cover and maintain 86°F, allowing the milk to ripen for 1 hour. Add the calcium chloride and gently whisk in for 1 minute, then add the rennet in the same way. Cover and let sit, maintaining 86°F for 30 to 45 minutes, or until the curds give a clean break.

3. Cut the curds into 1½-inch pieces and let sit for 5 minutes. Over low heat, slowly bring the curds to 102°F over a 40-minute period, stirring continuously to prevent them from matting. The curds will release more whey, Orm up, and shrink to the size of large lima beans.

4. Once 102°F is reached, remove from the heat, maintain the temperature, and let the curds rest undisturbed for 30 minutes. Heat 2 quarts of water to 120°F. Ladle o+ enough whey to expose the curds. Add enough hot water to bring the temperature to 104°F. Stir continuously for 15 minutes, or until the curds cling together when pressed in your hand.

5. Line a colander with damp butter muslin and place it over a bowl or bucket large enough to capture the whey, which can be discarded. Gently ladle the curds into the colander and rinse with cold non-chlorinated water to cool them. Let drain for 5 minutes, then sprinkle in 1 tablespoon of the salt and gently and thoroughly toss with your hands.

6.   Place a mat on a draining rack set over a tray, then set a 7-inch square Taleggio mold on the mat. Put the sack of rinsed curds in the mold and press the curds into the corners. Cover the top of the curds with the cloth tails and press with your hands to mat the curds. Let drain at room temperature for 6 hours for moist cheese, or 8 hours for a Xrmer cheese. Flip the cheese once halfway through this draining period.

7.   Remove the cheese from the mold and pat dry. Rub the surface of the cheese with the remaining 1 tablespoon of salt and place it back in the mold without the cloth. Return the mold to the mat on the draining rack for 12 hours, Dipping once in that time.

8.   Remove the cheese from the mold and place in a ripening box at 50°F to 55°F and 85 percent humidity for at least 2 weeks, Uipping the cheese daily for even ripening.

9.   After 1 week, wash with a simple brine solution twice a week for up to 2 months of ripening time. When the desired ripeness is reached, wrap and refrigerate until ready to eat.

23. Lemon vodka spirited goat

MAKES 1½ pounds

- 2 gallons pasteurized goat's milk
- 1 teaspoon MM 100 powdered mesophilic starter culture
- ¼ teaspoon Thermo B powdered thermophilic starter culture Geotrichum candidum 15 mold powder
- ¼ teaspoon calcium chloride diluted in ¼ cup cool nonchlorinated water

- 1 teaspoon liquid rennet diluted in ¼ cup cool nonchlorinated water
- Kosher salt (preferably Diamond Crystal brand) or cheese salt Pinch of Brevibacterium linens powder
- 1 cup Charbay Meyer Lemon Vodka or other lemon-infused vodka

1. In a nonreactive 10-quart stockpot, heat the milk over low heat to 90°F; this should take about 20 minutes. Turn off the heat.

2. Sprinkle both starters and a pinch of the mold powder over the milk and let rehydrate for 5 minutes. Mix well using a whisk in an up-and-down motion. Cover and maintain 90°F, allowing the milk to ripen for 45 minutes. Add the calcium chloride and gently whisk in for 1 minute, then add the rennet in the same way. Cover and let sit, maintaining 90°F for 30 to 45 minutes, or until the curds give a clean break.

3. Still maintaining 90°F, cut the curds into ½-inch pieces and let rest for 10 minutes. Gently stir the curds for 10 minutes, then let rest for 30 minutes. Slowly raise the temperature to 100°F over 30 minutes, stirring the curds every 5 minutes. Let the curds sit for about 10 minutes; they will sink to the bottom.

4. Ladle out enough whey to expose the curds, then gently ladle the curds into a colander lined with damp butter muslin and let drain for 5 minutes.

5. Line an 8-inch tomme mold or 7-inch square Taleggio mold with damp butter muslin and set on a draining rack. Transfer the curds to the mold, gently distributing and pressing into the mold with your hand. Cover the curds with the cloth tails and a follower and press at 3 pounds for 1 hour.

6. Remove the cheese from the mold, unwrap, Uip, and redress, then press at 5 pounds for 12 hours, Tipping once at 6 hours.

7. Make 2 quarts of saturated brine (see Brine Chart) and chill to 50°F to 55°F. Remove the cheese from the mold and cloth and place it in the brine to soak at 50°F to 55°F for 8 hours, Uipping at least once during the brining process.

8. Remove the cheese from the brine and pat it dry. Air-dry on a cheese mat at room temperature for 12 hours, or until the surface is dry.

9. Place the cheese on a mat in a ripening box and age at 50°F to 55°F and 90 percent humidity, ipping daily for 1 week. Each time you ip the cheese, wipe any moisture from the bottom, sides, and lid of the box.

10. After 1 week, begin washing the surface with bacterial wash. Twelve hours before the rst washing, prepare the solution by dissolving 1½ teaspoons of salt in 1 cup of cool nonchlorinated water in a sterilized glass jar. Add 1 pinch each of Geotrichum candidum mold powder and

B. linens powder, whisk to incorporate, cover, and store at 55°F.

11.   When ready to wash, pour 1½ tablespoons of the bacterial wash into a small bowl, preserving the rest for another washing. Dip a small piece of cheesecloth into the solution, squeeze out the excess, and rub it all over the entire surface of the cheese. Using a paper towel, wipe any excess moisture from the ripening box. Flip the cheese over and return it to the ripening box. Discard any bacterial wash left in the bowl.

12.   Wash the cheese twice a week for 2 months, alternating the bacterial wash with spirits. To wash with the vodka, pour a little vodka into a bowl, dip a small piece of cheesecloth in it, wring out, and rub it over the entire surface of the cheese.

13. Discard any vodka left in the bowl. The rind will become slightly sticky, and at 10 to 14 days a light orange color will develop, which will deepen as the cheese ages. At 2 months, the rind should be only slightly moist and the cheese should be soft to the touch in the center; it is now ready to eat. The cheese should be eaten within 3 months.

24. Époisses

MAKES Two ½-pound cheeses

- 1 gallon pasteurized whole cow's milk
- 1 teaspoon Meso II powdered mesophilic starter culture
- Pinch of Brevibacterium linens powder
- ¼ teaspoon calcium chloride diluted in ¼ cup cool nonchlorinated water
- 2 drops liquid rennet diluted in ¼ cup cool nonchlorinated water
- Kosher salt (preferably Diamond Crystal brand)
- 3 cups Marc de Bourgogne brandy, other similar pomace brandy, or grappa

1. In a nonreactive 10-quart stockpot, heat the milk over low heat to 86°F; this should take about 15 minutes. Turn oP the heat.

2. Sprinkle the starter and B. linens powder over the milk and let rehydrate for 5 minutes. Mix well using a whisk in an up-and-down motion. Cover and maintain 86°F, allowing the milk to ripen for 30 minutes. Add the calcium chloride and gently whisk in for 1 minute, then add the rennet in the same way. Cover and let the milk ripen for 4 hours at room temperature, until the curds give a clean break.

3. Over low heat, bring the curds back to 86°F. Cut the curds into ¾-inch pieces and let sit for 5 minutes. At this point the curds will be extremely soft.

4. Line two 4-inch Camembert molds with damp cheesecloth and set on a draining rack over a tray. Gently ladle the curds into the molds, cover with the cloth tails, and cover the entire setup with a kitchen towel. Let drain for 24 hours at room temperature, preferably in a warm spot in the kitchen. Once the drained curds have shrunk to half the height of the molds, Rip the cheeses over every 2 hours.

5. Remove the cheeses from the molds and cloth. Rub about 1 teaspoon of salt over the entire surface of each cheese. Air-dry at room temperature on a rack for 18 hours, until the surface is dry to the touch.

6.   Place the cheeses on a mat in a ripening box and age at 50°F and 90 percent humidity,

7.   ipping every 3 days for 6 weeks. Before you Rip the cheese the rst time, make a brine wash by dissolving 1 teaspoon of salt in ½ cup of boiled water and cooling it to 50°F to 55°F. Each time you ip the cheese, rst use a paper towel to wipe any moisture from the surface of the cheese, then wipe the entire surface of the cheese with a small piece of cheesecloth dipped in the brine wash. Discard any unused brine wash. Also use a paper towel to wipe any moisture from the bottom, sides, and lid of the ripening box each time you ip the cheese.

8.

9.   After the rst week, begin alternating the brine wash with a wash of diluted brandy (50 percent brandy and 50 percent water). Pour a little of the diluted brandy into a small dish, dip a small piece of cheesecloth in it, and rub it over the entire surface of the cheese. Discard any brandy wash left in the dish. At 3 weeks, begin alternating the brine wash with undiluted brandy.

10.   Continue washing and Zipping the cheese every 3 days for 6 weeks total. The rind will become slightly sticky and very aromatic, and at 10 to 14 days a pale orange color will develop; this will change to the color of the brandy used and deepen as the cheese ages. At 6 weeks, the rind should be moist but not sticky, the center of the cheese should feel very soft, and the paste should be runny. When the cheese is nearing the desired

ripeness, transfer it to the traditional wooden cheese box to nish (see headnote). Move the cheese to the refrigerator when fully ripened, and consume within 2 weeks.

25. Morbier

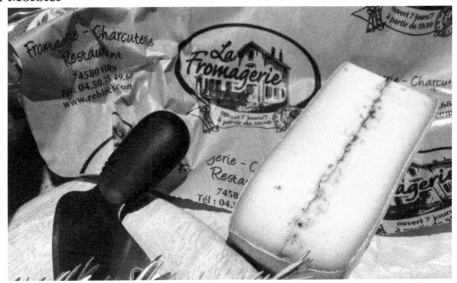

MAKES 1¾ pounds

- 2 gallons pasteurized whole cow's milk

- 1 teaspoon Meso II powdered mesophilic starter culture
- Brevibacterium linens powder
- ½ teaspoon calcium chloride diluted in ¼ cup cool nonchlorinated water
- ½ teaspoon liquid rennet diluted in ¼ cup cool nonchlorinated water
- ⅛ teaspoon vegetable ash mixed with ⅛ teaspoon Kne sea salt
- Kosher salt (preferably Diamond Crystal brand) or cheese salt

1. In a nonreactive 10-quart stockpot, heat the milk over low heat to 90°F; this should take about 20 minutes. Turn off the heat.

2. Sprinkle the starter and a pinch of B. linens powder over the milk and let rehydrate for 5 minutes. Mix well using a whisk in an up-and-down motion. Cover and maintain 90°F, allowing the milk to ripen for 1 hour. Add the calcium chloride and gently whisk in for 1 minute, then add the rennet in the same way.

3. Cover and let sit, maintaining 90°F for 30 minutes, or until the curds give a clean break.

4. Maintaining 90°F, cut the curds into ¾-inch pieces and let sit for 5 minutes. Over very low heat, slowly raise the temperature to 100°F over 30 minutes, stirring a few times. Let the curds settle for about 10 minutes. Using a measuring cup, remove about half of the whey and replace with enough 110°F water so the curds reach 104°F. Gently stir for 5 minutes, then let the curds settle.

5. Line 2 colanders with damp butter muslin, divide the curds between them, and let drain for 20 minutes. Line a draining rack with damp paper towels, extending the towels a few inches beyond the edges of the rack, and place an 8-inch tomme mold on top. Line the mold with damp butter muslin.

6. Transfer the contents of 1 colander of drained curds to the mold and press the curds into the edges with your hands. Wearing disposable gloves, use a ne-mesh strainer

to carefully dust the surface of the curds with ash to within ½ inch of the edge.

7. The dampened paper towels should catch any stray ash. Gently add the second batch of curds on top of the ash layer and press into the edges with your hands. Pull up the cloth and smooth out any wrinkles, then cover the curds with the cloth tails and the follower and press at 5 pounds for 1 hour. Remove the cheese from the mold, unwrap, ip, and redress, then press at 8 pounds for 12 hours or overnight.

8. Make 2 quarts of near-saturated brine (see Brine Chart) and chill to 50°F to 55°F. Remove the cheese from the mold and cloth and place in the brine to soak at 50°F to 55°F for 6 hours, Kipping at least once during the brining process.

9. Remove the cheese from the brine and pat dry. Place it on a cheese mat and air-dry at room temperature for 12 hours, or until the surface is dry to the touch.

10. Place the cheese on a mat in a ripening box to age at 50°F to 55°F and 85 to 90 percent humidity for 1 week. Flip daily, using a paper towel to wipe away any accumulated moisture in the box each time you tip the cheese.

11. After 1 week, wash the surface with bacterial wash. Twelve hours before this washing, prepare the solution: Boil ½ cup of water and let it cool in a glass jar, then add 1 teaspoon of kosher salt and stir to dissolve. Add a small pinch of B. linens powder, cover the jar with the lid, and

gently agitate to dissolve. Set aside at room temperature for the bacteria to rehydrate.

12.   When ready to wash, pour 1½ tablespoons of the bacterial wash into a small bowl, preserving the rest for another washing. Dip a small piece of cheesecloth into the solution, squeeze out the excess, and rub it over the entire surface of the cheese. Flip the cheese over and return it to the ripening box. Discard any bacterial wash left in the bowl.

13.   Two times a week, wash the cheese with a piece of cheesecloth dipped in simple brine (see Brine Chart) or rub the surface of the cheese with a soft brush dipped in brine. Repeat this process twice a week for 2 months,

14. Fipping the cheese each time. The rind will become slightly sticky, and at 10 to 14 days a light orange color will develop, deepening to a tan shade as the cheese ages.

15. After 3 weeks, the paste under the surface at the edges of the cheese will begin to feel soft. Continue to wash or brush for 2 months.

16. At 2 months, the rind should be only slightly moist (not sticky) and the cheese should be soft to the touch; it is now ready to eat. Or, wrap the cheese in cheese paper and refrigerate to age for up to 2 more months if desired.

26. Port salut

MAKES 1¼ pounds

- 6 quarts pasteurized whole cow's milk
- 1 teaspoon Meso II powdered mesophilic starter culture Brevibacterium linens powder
- 1 teaspoon calcium chloride diluted in ¼ cup cool nonchlorinated water
- 1 teaspoon liquid rennet diluted in ¼ cup cool nonchlorinated water Kosher salt (preferably Diamond Crystal brand) or cheese salt

1. In a nonreactive 8-quart stockpot, heat the milk over low heat to 90°F; this should take about 20 minutes. Turn off the heat.

2. Sprinkle the starter and a pinch of B. linens powder over the milk and let rehydrate for 5 minutes. Mix well using a whisk in an up-and-down motion. Cover and maintain 90°F, allowing the milk to ripen for 1 hour. Add the calcium chloride and gently whisk in for 1 minute, then add the rennet in the same way. Cover and let sit, maintaining 90°F for 30 minutes, or until the curds give a clean break.

3. Cut the curds into ½-inch pieces and let sit for 10 minutes. Meanwhile, heat 1 quart of water to 140°F. Ladle o about one-third of the whey and replace with enough 140°F water to bring the temperature to 92°F. Gently stir for 10 minutes, then let the curds settle for 10 minutes. Repeat the process, again removing one-third of the whey and this time adding enough 140°F water to bring the temperature to 98°F. Gently stir for 10 minutes, then let the curds settle for 15 minutes.

4. Line a colander with damp cheesecloth, ladle the curds into it, and let drain for 10 minutes. Line a 5-inch tomme mold with damp cheesecloth and set it on a draining rack. Transfer the drained curds to the lined cheese mold, pressing the curds into the edges with your hand.

5. Pull up the cloth and smooth out any wrinkles, cover the curds with the cloth tails and follower, and press at 5 pounds for 30 minutes. Remove the cheese from the mold, unwrap,Tip, and redress, then press at 8 pounds for 12 hours or overnight.

6.   Make 2 quarts of saturated brine (see Brine Chart) and chill to 50°F to 55°F. Remove the cheese from the mold and cloth and place in the brine to soak at 50°F to 55°F for 8 hours, Uipping at least once during the brining process.

7.   Remove the cheese from the brine and pat dry. Place on a cheese mat and air-dry at room temperature for 12 hours. Place the cheese on a mat in a ripening box and age at 50°F to 55°F and 90 to 95 percent humidity, ipping daily for 1 week. Each time you ip the cheese, wipe any moisture from the bottom, sides, and lid of the ripening box with a paper towel.

8.   After 1 week, begin washing the surface with bacterial wash. Twelve hours before the rst washing, prepare the solution: Boil ½ cup of water and let it cool in a glass jar, then add 1 teaspoon of kosher salt and stir to dissolve.

9. Add a small pinch of B. linens powder, cover the jar with the lid, and gently agitate to dissolve. Set aside at room temperature for the bacteria to rehydrate.

10.   When ready to wash, pour 1½ tablespoons of the bacterial wash into a small bowl, preserving the rest for

another washing. Dip a small piece of cheesecloth into the solution, squeeze out the excess, and rub the entire surface of the cheese. Flip the cheese over and return it to the ripening box. Discard any bacterial wash left in the bowl.

11. Repeat this process every 2 days, ipping the cheese each time. After you have washed the cheese with bacterial wash 4 times, switch to brine (1 teaspoon of salt dissolved in ½ cup of boiled water, cooled to 50°F to 55°F).

12.   The rind will become slightly sticky, and at 10 to 14 days a light yellow-orange color will develop; this color will deepen as the cheese ages.

13. Continue to wash and ripen for 4 weeks total. At this point the rind should be moist but not sticky and the center of the cheese should feel somewhat soft. Consume within 2 weeks of desired ripeness.

27. Reblochon

MAKES Two 1-pound cheeses

- 2 gallons pasteurized whole cow's milk
- 1 teaspoon Meso II powdered mesophilic starter culture
- ⅛ teaspoon Brevibacterium linens powder
- 1 teaspoon calcium chloride diluted in ¼ cup cool nonchlorinated water
- 1 teaspoon liquid rennet diluted in ¼ cup cool nonchlorinated water
- Kosher salt (preferably Diamond Crystal brand) or cheese salt

1. In a nonreactive 10-quart stockpot, heat the milk over low heat to 85°F; this should take about 15 minutes. Turn off the heat.

2.	Sprinkle the starter and B. linens powder over the milk and let rehydrate for 5 minutes. Mix well using a whisk in an up-and-down motion. Cover and maintain 85°F, allowing the milk to ripen for 30 minutes. Add the calcium chloride and gently whisk in for 1 minute, then add the rennet in the same way. Cover and let sit, maintaining 85°F for 30 minutes, or until the curds give a clean break.

3.	Still maintaining 85°F, cut the curds into ½-inch pieces and let sit for 5 minutes. Slowly warm the curds to 95°F over 30 minutes, stirring every 10 minutes, then remove from the heat and let the curds settle.

4.	Ladle out enough whey to expose the curds. Line two 5-inch tomme molds with damp cheesecloth and set them on a draining rack over a tray. Transfer the curds to the molds; you may have to mound them up in the molds, but they will all t in after 10 to 15 minutes of draining.

5.	Let drain for 15 minutes, then pull up the cloth and smooth out any wrinkles. Cover the curds with the tails of cloth and the followers. Let drain on the rack for 30 minutes, then Xip the cheeses, return them to the molds, and replace the followers. Flip every 20 minutes for 2 hours, then press at 5 pounds for 12 hours or overnight.

6.	Remove the cheeses from the molds and cloth. Sprinkle 1 teaspoon of salt on the top and bottom of each cheese. Place the cheeses on a mat in a ripening box and age at 55°F and 90 percent humidity, Qipping every other day.

7. Before you turn the cheese the Wrst time, make a brine wash: boil ½ cup of water and let it cool, then add 1 teaspoon of kosher salt and stir to dissolve. Store in the refrigerator. Each time you Uip the cheese, wipe the surface with a small piece of cheesecloth dipped in a small amount of brine wash.

8. The brine wash will control unwanted mold growth. Discard any unused brine wash and make a fresh batch each week. Also wipe away any moisture from the bottom, sides, and lid of the ripening box each time you ip the cheese.

9.   Continue Wipping and washing the cheese every 2 days for 2 to 6 weeks. At 10 to 14 days, a light yellow-orange color will develop, deepening as the cheese ages. At 4 weeks, the rind should be moist but not sticky and the center of the cheese should feel soft. Wrap the cheese in cheese paper, refrigerate when at the desired ripeness, and consume within 2 weeks of desired ripeness.

28. Taleggio

MAKES One 2-pound cheese or two 1-pound cheeses

- 2 gallons pasteurized whole cow's milk
- 1 teaspoon Meso II powdered mesophilic starter culture
- Pinch of Brevibacterium linens powder
- 1 teaspoon calcium chloride diluted in ¼ cup cool nonchlorinated water
- 1 teaspoon liquid rennet diluted in ¼ cup cool nonchlorinated water
- Kosher salt (preferably Diamond Crystal brand) or cheese salt

1. Heat the milk in a nonreactive 10-quart stockpot over low heat to 90°F; this should take 20 minutes. Turn off the heat.

2. Sprinkle the starter and B. linens powder over the milk and let rehydrate for 5 minutes. Mix well using a whisk in an up-and-down motion. Cover and maintain 90°F, allowing the milk to ripen for 1 hour. Add the calcium chloride and gently whisk in for 1 minute, then add the rennet in the same way. Cover and let sit, maintaining 90°F for 30 minutes, or until the curds give a clean break.

3. Still maintaining 90°F, cut the curds into ¾-inch pieces and let sit for 5 minutes. Gently stir the curds for 30 minutes, removing 2 cups of whey every 10 minutes. Then, let the curds rest undisturbed for 10 minutes.

4. Line one 7-inch square Taleggio mold or two 4-inch square bottomless cheese molds with damp cheesecloth and set on a draining rack over a tray. Gently ladle the curds into the molds, pressing them into the edges with your hand.

5. Cover with the tails of cloth and cover the entire setup with a kitchen towel. Let drain for 12 hours at room temperature, preferably in a warm spot in the kitchen. Every 2 hours, remove the cheese from the mold, unwrap, ip, and redress.

6.   Make 3 quarts of saturated brine (see Brine Chart) and chill to 50°F to 55°F. Remove the cheese from the mold and cloth and place in the brine to soak at 50°F to 55°F for 8 hours, Uipping at least once during the brining process.

7.   Remove the cheese from the brine and pat dry. Air-dry at room temperature on a cheese mat for 24 hours, or until the surface is dry to the touch. Place on a mat in a ripening box to age at 50°F and 90 percent humidity, Tipping every other day.

8. Before you ip the cheese the Krst time, make a brine wash: boil ½ cup of water and let it cool, then add 1 teaspoon of kosher salt and stir to dissolve. Store in the refrigerator. Each time you ip the cheese, wipe the surface with a small piece of cheesecloth dipped in a small amount of brine wash.

9. The brine wash will control unwanted mold growth. Discard any unused brine wash and make a fresh batch each week. Also wipe away any moisture from the bottom, sides, and lid of the ripening box each time you Wip the cheese.

10.   Flip and wash the cheese every 2 days for 4 to 5 weeks. At 10 to 14 days, a light yellow-orange color will develop, deepening as the cheese ages. At 4 to 5 weeks, the rind should be moist but not sticky and the center of the cheese should feel soft. Consume within 2 weeks of desired ripeness.

BLUE CHEESES

29. Bloomy Blue Log Chèvre

MAKES Two 6-ounce logs

- 1 gallon pasteurized goat's milk
- 1 teaspoon Aroma B powdered mesophilic starter culture
- ⅛ teaspoon Penicillium candidum mold powder
- Pinch of Geotrichum candidum 15 mold powder
- Pinch of Penicillium roqueforti mold powder
- 1 teaspoon calcium chloride diluted in ¼ cup cool nonchlorinated water
- 1 teaspoon liquid rennet diluted in ¼ cup cool nonchlorinated water
- 1 tablespoon Hne sea salt
- 1½ tablespoons vegetable ash

1. Heat the milk in a nonreactive 6-quart stockpot over low heat to 72°F; this should take 10 minutes. Turn off the heat.

2. Sprinkle the starter and mold powders over the milk and let rehydrate for 5 minutes. Mix well using a whisk in an up-and-down motion. Add the calcium chloride and gently whisk in for 1 minute, then add the rennet in the same way.

3. Cover and let sit, maintaining 72°F for 18 hours, or until the curds form a Xrm mass and the whey is coating on the top.

4. Place 2 Camembert or other round, straight-sided molds on a mat on a draining rack over a tray, and steady 2 cylindrical Saint-Maure molds inside them.

5. With a ladle or skimmer, gently cut ½-inch-thick slices of curds and layer them in the cylindrical molds to Oll. Let drain until more curds can be added to the molds. Do not be tempted to add another mold; the curds will compress as the whey drains out, making room for all of the curds.

6. Cover the molds, rack, and tray with a kitchen towel and let the cheeses drain for 24 hours at room temperature. Remove any accumulated whey a few times while draining, wiping out the tray when you do so. Flip the cheeses after 6 hours, or when they are Krm enough to handle, then Dip them a few more times during the 24

hours. At the end of 24 hours, the curds will have reduced to about half the height of the molds.

7.　　Once the cheeses have stopped draining and the curds have compressed to below the halfway point of the molds, remove the molds and sprinkle 2 teaspoons of the salt over the entire surface of each cheese. Set on the rack for 10 minutes to allow the salt to dissolve.

8.　　In a small bowl or jar, combine the vegetable ash with the remaining 1 teaspoon of salt. Wearing disposable gloves, use a Vne-mesh strainer to lightly dust the cheeses with vegetable ash, coating them completely. Gently pat the ash onto the surface of the cheeses.

9. Place the dusted cheeses at least 1 inch apart on a clean cheese mat in a ripening box. Cover the box loosely with the lid and let stand at room temperature for 24 hours. Let drain and wipe out any moisture from the box, then ripen the cheese at 50°F to 55°F and 90 percent humidity for 2 weeks.

10. For the first few days, adjust the lid to be slightly open for a portion of each day to maintain the desired humidity level. The surface of the cheese should appear moist but not wet.

11.　　Flip the cheeses one-quarter turn daily to maintain their log shape. After about 5 days, the rst signs of white fuzzy mold will appear. After 10 to 14 days, the cheeses will be fully coated in white mold. After 3 weeks, some of the dark ash will appear through the white mold. Left a bit longer, more dark ash will appear. After a total of 4 weeks from the start of ripening, wrap in cheese paper and store in the refrigerator. It is best to consume this cheese when it reaches your desired ripeness.

30. Blue gouda

MAKES 1½ pounds

- 2 gallons pasteurized whole cow's milk
- 1 teaspoon Meso II powdered mesophilic starter culture ⅛ teaspoon Penicillium roqueforti mold powder
- 1 teaspoon calcium chloride diluted in ¼ cup cool nonchlorinated water (omit if using raw milk)
- 1 teaspoon liquid rennet diluted in ¼ cup cool nonchlorinated water
- Kosher salt or cheese salt

1.   In a nonreactive 10-quart stockpot, heat the milk over low heat to 86°F; this should take 15 to 18 minutes. Turn off the heat.

2. Sprinkle the starter and mold powder over the milk and let rehydrate for 5 minutes. Mix in well using a whisk in an up-and-down motion. Cover and maintain 86°F, allowing the milk to ripen for 45 minutes. Add the calcium chloride and gently whisk in for 1 minute, then add the rennet in the same way.

3. Cover and let sit, maintaining 86°F for 30 minutes, or until the curds give a clean break.

4. Still maintaining 86°F, cut the curds into ½-inch pieces and let sit for 5 minutes. Then stir for 5 minutes and let stand for 5 minutes. Heat 2 quarts of water to 140°F and maintain that heat. When the curds sink to the bottom of the pot, ladle oL 2 cups of the whey, then add enough 140°F water to bring the curds to 92°F.

5. Gently stir for 10 minutes, then let the curds settle. Ladle o enough whey to expose the tops of the curds, then add enough 140°F water to bring the curds to 98°F. Gently stir for 20 minutes, or until the curds have shrunk to the size of small beans. Let the curds settle for 10 minutes; they will knit together in the bottom of the pot.

6. Warm a colander with hot water, then drain o the whey and place the knitted curds in the colander. Let drain for 5 minutes. Line a 5-inch tomme mold with damp cheesecloth and set it on a draining rack over a tray. Using your hands, break o 1-inch chunks of curd and distribute into the mold. Lightly press them into place to ll the gaps.

7. Pull the cloth up tight and smooth, cover the curds with the cloth tails and the follower, and press at 5 pounds for 30 minutes.

8. Remove the cheese from the mold, unwrap, Uip, and redress, then press at 10 pounds for 6 hours.

9. Make 3 quarts of saturated brine (see Brine Chart) and chill to 50°F to 55°F. Remove the cheese from the mold and cloth and place it in the brine to soak at 50°F to 55°F for 8 hours, Uipping it once during the brining.

10. Remove the cheese from the brine and pat dry. Place on a rack and air-dry at room temperature for 1 to 2 days, or until the surface is dry to the touch.

11. Place on a mat in a ripening box, cover loosely, and age at 50°F to 55°F and 85 percent humidity for 1 week, Ripping daily. Remove any unwanted mold with a small piece of cheesecloth dampened in a vinegar-salt solution.

12. Coat with wax and store at 50°F to 55°F and 75 percent humidity for at least 6 weeks and up to 4 months. The cheese will be ready to eat at 6 weeks.

31. Buttermilk blue

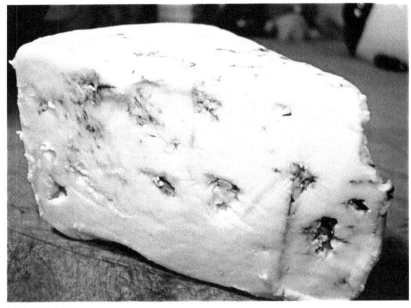

MAKES 10 ounces

- 2 quarts pasteurized whole cow's milk
- 1 quart cultured buttermilk, homemade (see variation on Crème Fraîche) or store-bought
- 2 cups heavy cream
- 1 teaspoon MM 100 powdered mesophilic starter culture Penicillium roqueforti mold powder
- 1 teaspoon calcium chloride diluted in ¼ cup cool nonchlorinated water
- 1 teaspoon liquid rennet diluted in ¼ cup cool nonchlorinated water

- 1½ teaspoons kosher salt (preferably Diamond Crystal brand), cheese salt, or Lne Pake sea salt

1. In a 6-quart stockpot over low heat, heat the milk, buttermilk, and cream to 90°F; this should take about 20 minutes. Turn off the heat.

2. Sprinkle the starter and a pinch of the mold powder over the milk and let rehydrate for 5 minutes. Mix in well using a whisk in an up-and-down motion. Cover and maintain 90°F, allowing the milk to ripen for 30 minutes. Add the calcium chloride and gently whisk in, then add the rennet in the same way. Cover and maintain 90°F for 1½ hours, or until the curds give a clean break.

3. Still maintaining 90°F, cut the curds into 1-inch pieces and let sit for 10 minutes. Then gently stir for 10 minutes to shrink the curds slightly and rm them up. Let stand for another 15 minutes, or until the curds sink to the bottom. Ladle o enough whey to expose the curds.

4. Line a colander with damp butter muslin and gently ladle the curds into it. Let drain for 10 minutes. Tie the corners of the cloth together to form a draining sack and hang for 20 minutes, or until the whey stops draining.

5. Line a 4-inch Camembert mold with damp butter muslin and place it on a rack over a tray. Gently ladle the curds into the mold, lling it to one-fourth its height and pressing down slightly with your hand to ll the gaps.

6.

7. Measure out ⅛ teaspoon of P. roqueforti powder. Lightly sprinkle the curds with one-third of the mold powder, then add more curds to Vll the mold halfway, again gently pressing to ll the gaps and sprinkling another one-third of the mold powder over the curds.

8. Repeat to Ull the mold with two more layers of curds and one of mold powder; the curds should come up to about 1 inch from the top of the mold. Pull the cloth up tight and smooth and cover the curds with the cloth tails. Let the cheese drain for 4 hours at room temperature, then unwrap, Dip, redress, and let drain for 4 more hours.

9. Carefully remove the cheese from the mold, unwrap, and sprinkle one side with ¾ teaspoon of the salt. Flip the cheese and place the cheese mold over it. The cheese will be fairly fragile, so handle it gently. Place it on a mat in a ripening box and sprinkle the remaining ¾ teaspoon of salt on the top.

10. Let drain for 5 hours, then remove the mold. Dry salt the sides of the cheese. Put the cheese in a ripening box, cover loosely with the lid, and age at 54°F and 75 percent humidity for up to 1 week, or until the whey stops draining. Flip the cheese daily, draining o any whey that may have accumulated in the ripening box and using a paper towel to wipe any moisture from the bottom, sides, and lid of the box.

11.   Once the whey has stopped draining, use a sterilized knitting needle or round skewer to pierce the cheese all the way through to the other side, four times horizontally and four times vertically. These air passages will encourage mold growth.

12.   Secure the lid of the ripening box and ripen at 50°F and 85 to 90 percent humidity. Blue mold should appear on the exterior after 10 days. Watch the cheese carefully, ipping it daily and adjusting the lid if the humidity increases and too much moisture develops.

13.   Over the next 2 weeks, pierce the cheese one or two more times in the same locations to ensure proper aeration and blue vein development. If any excessive or undesirable mold appears on the exterior of the cheese, rub it o with a small piece of cheesecloth dipped in a vinegar-salt solution.

14. Ripen for 6 weeks, rub o any excess mold with dry cheesecloth, then wrap the cheese in foil and store refrigerated for up to 3 more months or longer for a more pronounced Xavor.

32. Cambozola

MAKES Two 10-ounce cheeses

- 2 gallon pasteurized whole cow's milk
- 2 gallon pasteurized heavy cream
- 1 teaspoon Meso II or C101 powdered mesophilic starter culture
- ⅛ teaspoon Penicillium candidum mold powder
- 1 teaspoon calcium chloride diluted in ¼ cup cool nonchlorinated water
- 1 teaspoon liquid rennet diluted in ¼ cup cool nonchlorinated water

- ⅛ teaspoon Penicillium roqueforti mold powder
- 4 teaspoons kosher salt (preferably Diamond Crystal brand), cheese salt

1. Combine the milk and cream in a nonreactive 6-quart stockpot set in a 96°F water bath over low heat and gently warm to 86°F; this should take about 10 minutes. Turn off the heat.

2. Sprinkle the starter and P. candidum mold powder over the milk and let rehydrate for 5 minutes. Mix in well using a whisk in an up-and-down motion. Cover and maintain 86°F, allowing the milk to ripen for 30 minutes. Add the calcium chloride and gently whisk in, then add the rennet in the same way. Cover and let sit, maintaining 86°F for 1½ hours, or until the curds give a clean break.

3. Cut the curds into ½-inch pieces and gently stir for 5 minutes. Let the curds rest for 5 minutes.

4. Line a colander with damp cheesecloth and gently ladle the curds into it. Let drain for minutes.

5. Line 2 Saint-Maure molds with damp cheesecloth and set them on a draining rack over a tray. Using a skimmer, gently ladle the curds into the molds until half full. Sprinkle the top of each cheese with half of the P. roqueforti mold powder, then top o each mold with the remaining curds. Let drain for 6 hours at room temperature, draining o and wiping out any whey that collects.

6. Remove any accumulated whey a few times during draining, wiping out the tray when you do so. When the cheeses are rm enough to handle (after about 8 hours), unmold and unwrap them and discard the cheesecloth, then Hip them and return them to the unlined molds. Unmold and Lip one more time while the cheeses are draining. The cheeses should drain for 8 to 10 hours total.

7. Once the cheeses have stopped draining, remove them from the molds and place on a clean mat set in a clean, dry ripening box. Sprinkle 2 teaspoons of the salt over the tops of the cheeses and wait 5 minutes for the salt to dissolve. Flip the cheeses over and sprinkle the tops with the remaining 2 teaspoons of salt.

8. Cover the box loosely with its lid. Ripen at 50°F to 55°F and 90 percent humidity. High humidity is essential for making this cheese. Flip the cheeses daily, wiping away any whey that accumulates in the ripening box. When the cheeses are dry on the surface (after about 3 days), cover the box tightly to continue ripening.

9. Continue to ip the cheeses daily and remove any moisture in the box. After about 5 days, the rst signs of white fuzzy mold will appear. When the cheeses are fully coated in white mold (after about 8 days), aerate the center of each cheese by piercing horizontally from the sides through the center to the other side using a sterilized knitting needle or skewer.

10. There should be 8 to 10 piercings through each cheese to allow proper development of blue veins. Pierce again in the same places if any holes close up over the next 10 to 12 days.

11.   Wrap in cheese paper 10 to 12 days after piercing and return to the ripening box. The cheese will begin to soften within 1 week or so. After a total of 4 weeks from the start of ripening, the cheese should be ready to eat, or continue to ripen to 6 weeks in the refrigerator.

33. Coastal blue

MAKES Two 1-pound cheeses

- 2 gallons pasteurized whole cow's milk
- 1 teaspoon MM 100 powdered mesophilic starter culture
- ⅛ teaspoon Penicillium roqueforti mold powder
- ¼ teaspoon calcium chloride diluted in ¼ cup cool nonchlorinated water
- ¼ teaspoon liquid rennet diluted in ¼ cup cool nonchlorinated water
- 2 tablespoons coarse kosher salt (preferably Diamond Crystal brand)

1. In a nonreactive 10-quart stockpot set in a 96°F water bath over low heat, gently warm the milk to 86°F; this should take about 10 minutes. Turn off the heat.

2. Sprinkle the starter and the mold powder over the milk and let rehydrate for 5 minutes. Mix well using a whisk in an up-and-down motion. Cover and maintain 86°F, letting the milk ripen for 1 hour, stirring every once in a while. Add the calcium chloride and gently whisk in, then add the rennet in the same way. Cover and let sit, maintaining 86°F for 1 to 1½ hours, or until the curds give a clean break.

3. Cut the curds into ½-inch pieces and gently stir for 10 minutes, then let the curds settle to the bottom of the pot. Ladle out 2 quarts of whey and stir the curds for 5 more minutes.

4. Line a colander or strainer with damp butter muslin and gently ladle the curds into it. Let drain for 5 minutes. Line two 4-inch Camembert molds with damp cheesecloth and set them on a draining rack over a tray.

5. Ladle the curds into the molds, pull the cloth up around the curds and cover the top with the tails of the cloth, and let drain for 12 hours at room temperature. Flip the cheeses at least four times to ensure a uniform shape and appearance.

6.   Remove the cheeses from the molds and sprinkle 1 tablespoon of salt over the entire surface of each, coating them evenly. Gently pat the salt into the surface. Set the cheeses on a mat in a ripening box and age at 68°F to 72°F and 90 percent humidity. Set the lid ajar a little so there is some air movement. Flip the cheeses daily, wiping away any excess moisture from the box with a paper towel.

7.   After 2 days, use a sterilized knitting needle or round skewer to pierce each cheese all the way through to the other side, 4 times horizontally and 4 times vertically. These air passages will encourage mold growth.

8.   Place the cheeses back in the box and ripen at 50°F to 56°F and 85 percent humidity for 3 to 4 weeks. After 10 days, blue mold should start to appear. Flip the cheeses daily, wiping away any excess moisture from the box with a paper towel. Rub o any undesirable mold with a piece of cheesecloth dipped in a vinegar-salt solution and wrung to dry.

9. After su cient blue mold growth is achieved, wrap them in tightly in foil and refrigerate for up to 4 to 6 months.

34. Gorgonzola

MAKES 1½ pounds

- 6 quarts pasteurized whole cow's milk
- 1 teaspoon MM 100 powdered mesophilic starter culture
- 1 teaspoon calcium chloride diluted in ¼ cup cool nonchlorinated water
- ½ teaspoon liquid rennet diluted in ¼ cup cool nonchlorinated water
- ⅛ teaspoon Penicillium roqueforti mold powder
- Kosher salt

1. In a nonreactive 4-quart stockpot set in a 100°F water bath, gently warm 3 quarts of the milk to 90°F; this should take about 15 minutes. Turn off the heat.

2. Sprinkle half of the starter over the milk and let it rehydrate for 5 minutes. Mix in well using a whisk in an

up-and-down motion. Cover and maintain 90°F, letting the milk ripen for 30 minutes. Add half of the calcium chloride and gently whisk in, then add half of the rennet in the same way. Cover and let sit, maintaining 90°F for 30 minutes, or until the curds give a clean break.

3.   Cut the curds into ¾-inch pieces and let rest for 10 minutes, then gently stir for 20 minutes to Hrm up the curds slightly. Let rest for another 15 minutes, or until the curds sink to the bottom.

4.   Ladle out enough whey to expose the curds. Line a colander with damp cheesecloth and gently ladle the curds into it. Let drain for 5 minutes. Tie the corners of the cheesecloth together to form a draining sack and hang at 55°F to let drain for 8 hours or overnight.

5.   The next morning, make a second batch of curds in the same manner, using the other half of the milk, starter, calcium chloride, and rennet. Let the curds drain at 55°F for 6 hours. Before the second batch is done draining, bring the Krst batch to room temperature.

6.   Untie the sacks and, keeping the batches separate, break the curds into 1-inch chunks. Line a 4-inch Camembert mold with damp cheesecloth and place it on a draining rack.

7. Using your hands, line the bottom and sides of the mold with a thin layer of the second batch of curds. Press down slightly to Fill the gaps. Layer half of the curds from the

first batch in the mold and gently press down to ll the gaps.

8. Sprinkle the top with one-third of the P. roqueforti mold powder, then repeat the process two more times until the mold is Filled with four layers of curds, alternating rst-batch and second-batch curds and Finishing with second-batch curds. The mold should be Filled to about 1 inch from the top.

9. Pull the cheesecloth up around the curds and cover the top with the tails of the cloth and the follower. Press at 5 pounds for 2 hours, then unmold, unwrap, ip, and redress.

10. Press at 8 pounds for 2 hours. Press at 8 pounds for 6 more hours, unwrapping, ipping, and redressing every 2 hours.

11. Carefully remove the cheese from the mold, unwrap, and sprinkle one side with ¾ teaspoon of salt. Flip the cheese over and place the cheese mold over it. The cheese will be fairly fragile, so handle it gently. Place it on a mat in a ripening box and sprinkle ¾ teaspoon of salt over the top. Let drain for 5 hours, then ip the cheese again. Repeat this process once a day for 3 more days, sprinkling a pinch of salt on each side the rst time you ip it each day, then draining for 5 hours and ipping once again. Each time you Rip the cheese, drain any accumulated whey and wipe the box dry with a paper towel.

12. After the 4 days of salting, Dipping, and draining, remove the mold and cover the ripening box loosely with the lid. Age at 50°F and 75 percent humidity for up to 2 weeks, or until the whey stops draining. Flip the cheese daily, removing any whey that accumulates in the ripening box and wiping any moisture from the sides of the box.

13. Once the whey has stopped draining, use a sterilized knitting needle or round skewer to pierce the cheese all the way through to the other side, 4 times horizontally and 4 times vertically. These air passages will encourage mold growth.

14. Secure the lid of the ripening box and ripen at 50°F and 85 to 90 percent humidity. Blue mold should appear on the exterior after 10 days. Watch the cheese carefully, turning it daily and adjusting the lid if the humidity increases and too much moisture develops. Remove any unwanted mold with a piece of cheesecloth dipped in a vinegar-salt solution.

15. Over the 2 weeks after the initial piercing, pierce the cheese one or two more times in the same locations to ensure proper aeration and blue vein development.

16. Ripen for 2 months, then wrap the cheese in foil and store refrigerated for 1 to 3 more months.

35. Roquefort

MAKES 1 pound

- 2 quarts pasteurized whole cow's milk
- 2 quarts heavy cream
- 1 teaspoon MA 4001 powdered mesophilic starter culture
- 1 teaspoon mild lipase powder diluted in ¼ cup cool nonchlorinated water 20 minutes before using (optional)
- 1 teaspoon calcium chloride diluted in ¼ cup cool nonchlorinated water (omit if using raw milk)
- 1 teaspoon liquid rennet diluted in ¼ cup cool nonchlorinated water
- ⅛ teaspoon Penicillium roqueforti mold powder
- 1½ teaspoons kosher salt (preferably Diamond Crystal brand) or Une Eake sea salt

1. In a nonreactive 6-quart stockpot set in a 100°F water bath, combine the milk and cream and gently warm to

90°F; this should take about 15 minutes. Turn off the heat.

2.   Sprinkle the starter over the milk and let rehydrate for 5 minutes. Mix well using a whisk in an up-and-down motion. Cover and maintain 90°F, allowing the milk to ripen for few minutes. Add the lipase, if using, and gently whisk in, then gently whisk in the calcium chloride and then the rennet. Cover and let sit, maintaining 90°F for 2 hours or until the curds give a clean break.

3.   Cut the curds into 1-inch pieces and let rest for 15 minutes, then gently stir to rm up the curds slightly. Let rest for another 15 minutes, or until the curds sink to the bottom.

4.   Ladle out enough whey to expose the curds. Line a colander with damp cheesecloth and gently ladle the curds into it. Let drain for 10 minutes. Tie the corners of the cheesecloth together to form a draining sack and hang at room temperature to let drain for 30 minutes, or until the whey stops dripping.

5.   Set a 4-inch Camembert mold on a draining rack and line it with damp cheesecloth. Using your hands, layer one-fourth of the curds into the mold. Gently press down to ll in the gaps.

6.   Sprinkle the top of the curds with one-third of the P. roqueforti mold powder, then repeat the process until the

mold is lled, Hnishing with a layer of curds. The mold should be lled to about 1 inch from the top.

7. Let drain at room temperature for 8 hours. Once the curds have Irmed enough to handle, after about 4 hours of draining, tip the cheese a time or two, keeping it in its cheesecloth. After 8 hours, remove the cheese from the mold, unwrap, tip, and redress, then let drain for 16 hours at room temperature.

8. After 24 hours of draining, carefully remove the cheese from the mold, sprinkle one side with ¾ teaspoon of the salt, then Qip it over and place it on a mat in a ripening box.

9. Sprinkle the remaining ¾ teaspoon of salt over the top. The cheese will be fairly fragile at this point, so handle it gently.

10. Cover the box loosely and ripen the cheese at 50°F to 55°F and 85 to 90 percent humidity. Flip the cheese daily for 1 week, draining any accumulated liquid in the ripening box and using a paper towel to wipe any moisture from the box.

11. After 1 week, use a sterilized knitting needle or round skewer to pierce the cheese all the way through to the other side 4 times horizontally and 4 times vertically.

12. These passages will encourage mold growth. Continue to ripen at 50°F to 55°F and 85 to 90 percent humidity. Blue mold should appear on the exterior after 10 days.

13. Once the cheese has stopped draining whey, secure the box's lid to control the humidity. Flip the cheese daily and adjust the lid if the humidity increases and too much moisture develops.

14. Over the 2 weeks after the intial piercing, pierce one or two more times in the same locations to ensure proper aeration and blue vein development. Remove any excessive or unwanted mold with a piece of cheesecloth dipped in a vinegar-salt solution.

15. Ripen the cheese for 6 to 8 weeks. When it reaches the desired creamy texture, wrap it in foil and store it, refrigerated, for up to 4 more months.

36. Stilton

MAKES 1 pound

- 1 gallon pasteurized whole cow's milk
- 1 cup heavy cream
- Penicillium roqueforti mold powder
- 1 teaspoon C101 or Meso II powdered mesophilic starter culture
- 1 teaspoon calcium chloride diluted in ¼ cup cool nonchlorinated water
- 1 teaspoon liquid rennet diluted in ¼ cup cool nonchlorinated water

- 4 teaspoons kosher salt

1. In a nonreactive 6-quart stockpot, heat the milk and cream over low heat to 86°F; thisshould take about 15 minutes. Turn off the heat.

2. Sprinkle ⅛ teaspoon of the mold powder and the starter over the milk and let rehydrate for 5 minutes. Mix well using a whisk in an up-and-down motion. Cover and maintain 86°F, allowing the milk to ripen for 30 minutes. Add the calcium chloride and gently whisk in, then add the rennet in the same way. Cover and let sit, maintaining 86°F for 1½ hours, or until the curds give a clean break.

3. Using a skimmer, slice the curds into ½-inch-thick slabs. Line a colander with damp cheesecloth and set it over a bowl about the same size as the colander.

4. Transfer the curd slices to the colander; the curds should be sitting in the whey caught in the bowl. Cover the colander; maintain 86°F for 1½ hours. Then tie the corners of the cheesecloth together to form a draining sack and hang to let drain at room temperature for 30 minutes, or until the whey stops dripping.

5. Set the sack on a cutting board, open the cheesecloth, and gently press down on the curds, forming them into a brick shape. Redress the curds in the same cheesecloth and place on a draining rack. Press them at 8 pounds for 8 hours or overnight at room temperature.

6.   Remove the curds from the cheesecloth and break them into approximately 1-inch pieces. Place the curds in a bowl, add the salt, and gently toss to combine.

7.   Line a 4½-inch-diameter round cheese mold with damp cheesecloth and set it on a draining rack. Layer half of the curds into the mold. Sprinkle the top with a pinch of P. roqueforti mold powder, then layer the remaining curds in the mold.

8. Fold the tails of the cloth over the curds, set the follower in place, and let drain at room temperature for 4 days. Flip every 20 minutes for the rst 2 hours, every 2 hours for the next 6 hours, and once a day for the next 4 days. Remove any accumulated whey each time you ip the cheese.

9.   After the 4 days of draining, remove the cheese from the mold and cloth and place it on a clean mat in a dry ripening box. Cover the box loosely with the lid and ripen the cheese at 50°F to 55°F and 85 to 90 percent humidity. High humidity is essential for making this cheese.

10.   Flip the cheese daily for 1 week, removing any whey that accumulates in the ripening box and wiping any moisture from the box. Wipe the rind daily with cheesecloth soaked

11. in a simple brine solution (see Brine Chart) for the rst week. When the cheese is dry on the surface, secure the lid of the ripening box tightly and continue to ripen at

50°F to 55°F and 90 percent humidity, Qipping once or twice a week.

12. After 2 weeks, the cheese should have developed a slightly moldy exterior. At 4 months, wrap the cheese in foil and store refrigerated for up to 2 more months.

VEGAN CHEESE

37. Cashew cheddar

- 1 cup raw cashews
- 1 cup filtered water
- 1 teaspoon Himalayan salt
- ¼ cup modified tapioca starch
- Beta-carotene squeezed from 2 gel caps
- **1/4** cup refined coconut oil, plus more for greasing the pan
- 1½ teaspoo**ns** agar-agar powder
- Place the cashews in filtered water in a small bowl. Cover and refrigerate overnight.

a) Drain the cashews. In the pitcher of a Vitamix, place the cashews, water, modified tapioca starch, beta-carotene, coconut oil, and agar-agar powder.

b) Blend on high speed until smooth.

c) Oil a 4.5 x 1-inch round springform pan with coconut oil.

d) Transfer the cashew mixture to a saucepan and heat on medium-low, stirring continuously , until it becomes thick and cheese-like in consistency. (You can use a thermometer and heat the mixture to about 145 degrees F. See here for tips on this technique.)

e) At this stage, you can spread this warm, thick cheese onto toasted bread for a delicious sandwich. or you can fold the cheese into the prepared mold .and set it aside to cool.

f) Refrigerate the cheese overnight to set up.

g) Run a knife around the inside edge of the mold. Release the buckle on the spring form pan and, using the flat edge of a large knife, release the cheese from the bottom metal round.

h) Transfer to a cutting board. Using a sharp knife, slice the cheese and serve

38. Smoked Gouda

- 1/4 cup raw cashews
- 1/4 cup raw almonds
- 1/4 cup refined coconut oil, plus more for greasing
- 1 cup filtered water
- 1/4 cup modified tapioca starch
- 1 drop beta-carotene, squeezed out of the gel cap
- 1 teaspoon Himalayan salt
- 2½ tablespoons agar-agar flakes
- 1 teaspoon liquid smoke
a) Place the cashews in filtered water in a small bowl. Cover and refrigerate overnight. Place the almonds in filtered water in a small bowl. Cover and refrigerate overnight.
b) Lightly oil a 4-inch springform pan with coconut oil.

c) Drain the cashews.

d) Bring 4 cups of water to a boil in a medium saucepan over medium-high heat. Add the almonds and blanch them for 1 minute. Drain the almonds in a colander and remove the skins with your fingers (you can compost the skins).

e) In the pitcher of a Vitamix, place the cashews, almonds, water, the modified tapioca starch, beta-carotene, coconut oil, salt, and agar-agar.

f) Blend on high speed for 1 minute or until smooth.

g) Transfer the mixture to a saucepan and heat over medium-low heat, stirring continuously, until it becomes thick and cheese-like in consistency. (You can use a thermometer and heat the mixture to about 145 degrees F. See here for tips on this technique.)

h) Add in the liquid smoke and mix with a rubber spatula to incorporate well.

i) Pour the cheese into the prepared spring form pan. Smooth the cheese with the back of a spoon coated with coconut oil. Let the mixture cool, then cover it with a parchment paper round cut to the size of the cheese mold. Transfer the cheese to the fridge overnight to set up.

j) Run a sharp knife around the inside edge of the pan. Release the buckle and remove the ring of the mold. Using the flat edge of a large knife, separate the cheese from the bottom metal round and transfer to a cutting board. With a very sharp knife, slice the cheese and serve

39. Mozzarella balls in brine

- 1 cup raw cashews
- 1 cup raw almonds

BRINE

- 12 cups filtered water
- 2 tablespoons to ¼ cup Himalayan pink salt
- 1 cup filtered water
- 1/4 cup modified tapioca starch
- 1/4 cup refined coconut oil
- 1 teaspoon Himalayan salt
- 2½ tablespoons agar-agar flakes or 1½ teaspoons agar-agar powder

1. Place the cashews in filtered water in a small bowl. Cover and refrigerate overnight.

2. Rinse the almonds well. Place them in water in a small bowl. Cover and refrigerate overnight.
3. Prepare a brine solution by bringing the water to a boil in a large saucepan over high heat and adding the salt until it dissolves.
4. Transfer the brine to a ceramic bowl and place in the freezer.
5. Bring 4 cups water to a boil in a medium saucepan over medium-high heat. Add the almonds and blanch them for 1 minute. Drain the almonds in a colander and remove the skins with your fingers (you can compost the skins).

6. Drain the cashews. In the bowl of a Vitamix, place the cashews, almonds, water, modified tapioca starch, coconut oil, salt, and agar-agar.
7. Blend on high speed for 1 minute or until smooth.
8. Transfer the mixture to a saucepan and, stirring continuously , heat over medium-low heat until it becomes thick and cheese-like in consistency. (You can use a thermometer and heat the mixture to about 145 degrees F. See here for tips on this technique.)

9. Scoop the warm cheese from the saucepan with an ice cream scooper and drop it into the brine.

10. Add 1 cup of ice to the cheese in brine mixture. Cover and transfer to the fridge and refrigerate overnight.

40. Cashew-almond mozzarella

- 1 cup raw cashews
- 1 cup almonds
- 1 teaspoon apple cider vinegar
- 1 teaspoon Celtic sea salt
- One 15-ounce can coconut milk
- 1/4 cup refined coconut oil
- 1 cup filtered water
- ½ cup agar-agar flakes
1. Place the cashews in filtered water in a small bowl. Cover and refrigerate overnight.

2. Rinse the almonds well. Place them in water in a small bowl. Cover and refrigerate overnight.
3. Line two 6-inch rectangular nonstick molds with plastic wrap, leaving enough excess plastic wrap hanging over the sides to wrap the mixture once it's cooled.

4. Bring 4 cups of water to a boil in a medium saucepan over medium-high heat. Add the almonds and blanch them for 1 minute. Drain the almonds in a colander and remove the skins with your fingers (you can compost the skins). Drain the cashews. In the bowl of a food processor, place the almonds and cashews and pulse until they are mealy in texture. Add the vinegar and salt. Pulse again a few times to combine.

5. In a small saucepan over medium heat, combine the coconut milk, coconut oil, and water. When the mixture is warmed through, add the agar-agar flakes and stir constantly until the agar-agar is dissolved.

6. With the motor running, pour the mixture into the food processor tube and blend until the mixture is creamy. Stop the motor, remove the lid, and scrape down the sides. Process again to make sure the mixture gets incorporated well. This can also be done in the Vitamix for a smoother texture.

7. Pour the mixture into the prepared molds and let cool on the counter. After the cheese has cooled, cover it with the excess plastic wrap and refrigerate for 24 hours or until firm.

8. Turn the cheese out of the molds and slice.Use as a pizza topping or inside a tomato basil panini!

41. Vegan Provolone

- 1 cup raw cashews
- 1 cup filtered water
- 1/4 cup refined coconut oil, plus more for greasing the pan
- 1/4 cup modified tapioca starch
- 2 drops beta-carotene, squeezed out of the gel cap
- 1 teaspoon white truffle oil
- 1 teaspoon Himalayan salt
- 1½ teaspoons agar-agar powder or 2½ tablespoons agar-agar flakes

1. Place the cashews in filtered water in a small bowl. Cover and refrigerate overnight.

2. Lightly oil a 4.5 x 1.5-inch springform pan with coconut oil.
3. Drain the cashews. In the pitcher of a Vitamix, place the cashews, water, modified tapioca starch, beta-carotene, coconut oil, truffle oil, salt, and agar-agar. Blend on high speed for 1 minute or until smooth.
4. Transfer the mixture to a small saucepan over medium-low heat and stir continuously until it becomes thick and cheese-like in consistency. (You can use a thermometer and heat the mixture to about 145 degrees F. See here for tips on this technique.)

5. Pour the cheese into the prepared springform pan. Let it cool. Cover with a parchment round cut to the size of the mold, then transfer to the fridge overnight to set up
6. Turn the cheese out of the mold and place on a serving plate. Using a very sharp knife, slice it and eat it with Kale Chip

42. Macadamia nut herbed goat cheese

- 2 cups raw macadamia nuts
- 1 capsule acidophilus (3-billion-active-culture strain)
- 1 teaspoon plus ⅛ teaspoon Celtic sea salt
- 1/4 cup coconut milk
- 2 teaspoons refined coconut oil
- 1 teaspoon Himalayan salt
- 2 tablespoons Greek spices or za'atar (a blend of thyme, oregano, and marjoram)

1. In the pitcher of a Vitamix, place the macadamia nuts, acidophilus, ½ teaspoon Celtic sea salt, coconut milk, coconut oil, and the Himalayan salt. Blend on medium speed, using the plunger to evenly distribute the mixture.

2. Transfer the mixture to the center of an 8-inch piece of cheesecloth. Gather the edges together and tie off your

bundle with string. Place the cheese bundle in the dehydrator and dehydrate at 90 degrees F for 24 hours.

3. After the aging is complete, open the cheese bundle and, using an ice cream scooper, remove all the cheese from the cloth and place it (including the rind and center) in the bowl of a food processor. Whip until light and fluffy.

4. Adjust the seasonings to taste. If the taste is too mild, add the remaining ⅛ teaspoon Celtic sea salt.

5. Turn the cheese out onto a work surface and divide it in half. Lay one half in an 8-inch piece of wax paper. Roll the cheese inside the wax paper, moving back and forth to create a log. Repeat with the second half.

6. After the shape is set, even out the ends and gently roll and press in the herbs. Gently wrap the logs in cheesecloth. Transfer to the refrigerator for 2 hours. Serve.

43. Ahimsa goat cheese

- 2 cups almonds
- 3½ teaspoons apple cider vinegar, plus more as needed
- 1 teaspoon Celtic sea salt, plus more as needed
- ½ cup coconut milk
- 1 teaspoon refined coconut oil

1. Soak the almonds for at least 8 hours in filtered water. To sprout them, rinse the almonds with water twice a day for the next 48 hours. You can store them, covered with a piece of cheesecloth, in a cool, dry place. But make sure you drain the water from them completely each time you rinse them. Or, if desired, you can skip the sprouting step and just use soaked almonds. Your cheese will still be delicious.

2. Bring 4 cups of water to a boil in a medium saucepan over medium-high heat. Add the sprouted almonds and quickly blanch them, for 1 minute. Drain the almonds in a

colander and remove the skins with your fingers (you can compost the skins).

3. In the pitcher of a Vitamix, place the almonds, vinegar, salt, coconut milk, and coconut oil. Blend on medium speed, using the plunger to evenly distribute the mixture.

4. Transfer the mixture to the center of an 8-inch piece of cheesecloth. Gather the edges and tie them into a bundle with string. Place the cheesecloth bundle in the dehydrator and dehydrate at 90 degrees F for 19 to 24 hours.

5. After the aging is complete, open the cheesecloth bundle and, using an ice cream scooper, scoop the cheese into the bowl of a food processor. Whip until light and fluffy.

6. Adjust the seasonings to taste. If the taste is too mild, add another ⅛ teaspoon vinegar and ⅛ teaspoon salt.

7. Turn the cheese out onto wax paper. Divide the cheese into two equal parts. Roll the cheese inside the wax paper, moving back and forth to create two individual logs.

8. Enjoy with my Beet Goat Cheese Salad or with your favorite gluten-free crackers.

44. Gorgonzola blue cheese

- 4 cups raw cashews
- Coconut oil, for greasing the molds
- 1 capsule acidophilus (3-billion-active-culture strain)
- ¾ cup coconut milk
- 1 teaspoon Himalayan salt
- ¼ to ½ teaspoon spirulina or frozen liquid spirulina
1. Place the cashews in filtered water in a small bowl. Cover and refrigerate overnight.

2. Lightly oil two 4-inch cheese molds or one 6-inch cheese mold with coconut oil.
3. Drain the cashews. In the bowl of a Vitamix, place the cashews, acidophilus, coconut milk, and salt. Blend on

medium speed, using the plunger to evenly distribute the mixture until smooth.

4. Transfer the mixture to a small bowl and sprinkle with the powdered spirulina or break off small chunks of live frozen spirulina and randomly drop them over the cheese mixture. Using a small rubber spatula, marble the spirulina through the mixture to create blue-green veins.

5. Transfer the mixture to the prepared cheese molds and place them in the dehydrator topped with parchment paper rounds cut to fit the tops of the molds.

6. Dehydrate at 90 degrees F for 24 hours.

7. Transfer the molds to the fridge overnight.

8. Remove the cheese from the molds and enjoy, or place the cheese inside a humidifier or wine cooler for 1 to 3 weeks. Rub the outside with fine sea salt every few days to prevent black mold from appearing. The taste of the cheese will continue to develop as it ages.

45. Chipotle cheddar

- 1½ cups raw cashews
- 1/4 cup Irish moss
- ½ cup filtered water
- 1 teaspoon refined coconut oil
- ½ teaspoon chipotle chili from a jar, plus 1 tablespoon oil from the jar
- ½ teaspoon Celtic sea salt, plus more to taste
- 2 tablespoons nutritional yeast
1. Place the cashews in filtered water in a small bowl. Cover and refrigerate overnight.
2. Rinse the Irish moss very well in a colander until all the sand is removed and the smell of the ocean is gone. Then place it in water in a small bowl. Cover and refrigerate overnight.
3. Drain the Irish moss and place it in the bowl of a Vitamix with the water. Blend on high speed for 1 minute or until

it is emulsified. Measure out 2 tablespoons and reserve the rest.

4. Drain the cashews. In a clean pitcher of a Vitamix, place the cashews, the emulsified Irish moss, the coconut oil, chipotle chili, chipotle oil, salt, and nutritional yeast. Blend on medium speed, using the plunger to evenly distribute the ingredients until smooth.

5. Adjust the salt to taste. Spoon the mixture into the center of your tamale before wrapping. Olé!

46. Cashew bleu cheese

- 2 cups raw cashews
- 1/4 cup Irish moss
- ½ cup filtered water
- 1 tablespoon nutritional yeast 1½ teaspoons Celtic sea salt
- 2 teaspoons refined coconut oil
- 1 teaspoon garlic powder
- 1 capsule acidophilus (3-billion-active-culture strain)
- 1/4 cup aquafaba (water from a 15.5-ounce can of garbanzo beans)
- ½ teaspoon powdered spirulina or frozen live spirulina

1. Place the cashews in filtered water in a small pitcher. Cover and refrigerate overnight.

2. Rinse the Irish moss very well in a colander until all of the sand is removed and the smell of the ocean is gone. Then place it in filtered water in a small bowl. Cover and refrigerate overnight.

3. Drain the Irish moss and place it in the bowl of a Vitamix along with the water. Blend on high speed for 1 minute or until it is emulsified. Measure out 2 tablespoons and reserve the rest.

4. Drain the cashews. In a clean pitcher of the Vitamix, place the cashews, emulsified Irish moss, the nutritional yeast, salt, coconut oil, garlic powder, acidophilus, and aquafaba.

5. Blend on medium speed, using the plunger to evenly distribute the mixture. Transfer the mixture to a cheese mold.

6. Sprinkle the spirulina over the cheese and, using a small spatula, marble it through in all directions. Do not overmix or your cheese will turn green.

7. Place the cheese mold in the dehydrator and dehydrate at 90 degrees F for 24 hours. Refrigerate overnight.

8. Serve, or store in a humidifier or wine cooler for up to 3 weeks.

47. Vegan Burrata

MAKES APPROXIMATELY 2 CUPS

- 2 cups raw almonds
- 1 tablespoon apple cider vinegar
- 1 teaspoon Himalayan salt
- 1/4 cup coconut milk plus 1 cup for soaking
- 1 teaspoon coconut oil

1. Soak the almonds for at least 8 hours in filtered water. To
   sprout them, rinse the almonds with filtered water twice a
   day for the next 48 hours. You can store them, covered
   with a piece of cheesecloth, in a cool, dry place. But make

sure you drain the water from them completely each time you rinse them. Or if desired you can skip the sprouting step and just use soaked almonds. Your cheese will still be delicious.

2. Bring 4 cups of water to a boil in a medium saucepan over medium-high heat. Add the almonds and quickly blanch them, for 1 minute. Drain the almonds in a colander and remove the skins with your fingers (you can compost them).

3. In the pitcher of a Vitamix, place the almonds, vinegar, salt, ½ cup coconut milk, and the coconut oil. Blend on medium speed, using the plunger to evenly distribute the mixture until well incorporated and smooth.

4. Transfer the ingredients to the center of an 8-inch piece of fine cheesecloth. Gather the edges and tie them into a bundle with string. Hang the cheese bundle on a hook on the wall or on the underside of a cabinet. Place a small dish beneath it to catch the liquid. Hang overnight or until a soft darkened rind forms.

5. Place the cheesecloth bundle in a small bowl and add the remaining 1 cup of coconut milk. Cover and soak in the refrigerator for 3 to 5 days.

6. Before serving, cut the cheese into slices and arrange on some fresh greens with diced tomatoes. Try pouring 1 tablespoon of the soaking coconut milk right over the top of the slices. Drizzle some high-quality olive oil and balsamic vinegar over your gourmet creation, garnish with some fresh ground pepper, and serve. Then fall down on the floor in ecstasy. You're welcome.

48. Japanese miso cheese

MAKES 2 CUPS CHEESE

- 1 cup raw cashews
- 1 cup fresh coconut meat from a brown coconut (do not substitute with coconut flakes)
- ⅔ cup aquafaba (liquid from canned garbanzo beans)
- 1 tablespoon coconut oil, plus more for greasing the cheese molds
- 2 fermented black garlic cloves
- 1 tablespoon chickpea miso paste
- 1 tablespoon nutritional yeast

- 1 teaspoon apple cider vinegar
- 1 small seaweed sprig, any variety
- Pinch of large-grain Celtic sea salt

1. Place the cashews in filtered water in a small bowl. Cover and refrigerate overnight.
2. In the bowl of a food processor pulse the fresh coconut pieces until mealy in texture. Cover and refrigerate until ready to use.
3. Lightly oil one 4-inch round cheese mold with coconut oil.
4. Drain the cashews. In the pitcher of a Vitamix, place the cashews, coconut, aquafaba, and coconut oil. Blend on medium speed, using the plunger to evenly distribute the mixture until well incorporated and smooth. You may have to stop and scrape down the sides with a rubber spatula and then start again.

5. Transfer the cheese to the prepared cheese mold. Place the cheese mold in the dehydrator and dehydrate at 90 degrees F for 24 hours.

6. Remove the cheese from the mold and place in the bowl of a food processor. Add the garlic, miso, nutritional yeast, and vinegar. Process for 1 minute or until smooth. Transfer the mixture to a small decorative serving dish. Alternatively, transfer it into the prepared mold and refrigerate for 24 hours.

49. Whipped cashew ricotta

MAKES 2 CUPS

- 2 cups raw cashews
- 1/4 cup Irish moss
- ¾ cup filtered water
- 1 teaspoon rejuvelac
- 2 teaspoons fresh lemon juice
- 2 tablespoons aquafaba
- 1 teaspoon Celtic sea salt

1. Place the cashews in filtered water in a small bowl. Cover and refrigerate overnight.

2. Rinse the Irish moss very well in a colander until all of the sand is removed and the smell of the ocean is gone. Then place it in water in a small bowl. Cover and refrigerate overnight.
3. Drain the Irish moss and place it in the pitcher of a Vitamix with ½ cup water. Blend on high speed for 1 minute or until it is emulsified. Measure out 2 tablespoons and reserve the rest.

4. In a clean bowl of the Vitamix, place the cashews, emulsified Irish moss, rejuvelac, remaining ¼ cup water, and salt. Blend on medium speed, using the plunger to evenly distribute the mixture, stopping and starting until everything is well incorporated.
5. Transfer the cheese to the center of an 8-inch piece of fine cheesecloth. Gather the edges and tie them into a bundle with string.

6. Place the cheesecloth bundle in the dehydrator and dehydrate at 90 degrees F for 24 hours.
7. Transfer the cheese to the bowl of a food processor and pulse until the texture is light and fluffy.

50. Coconut cashew cheese

MAKES TWO 4-INCH ROUNDS

- 2 cups raw cashews
- 2 tablespoons coconut oil, plus more for greasing the cheese molds
- 2 cups fresh coconut meat from a brown coconut (do not substitute with coconut flakes)
- 1/4 cup aquafaba (liquid from canned garbanzo beans)
- 1 teaspoon Himalayan salt Edible flower petals, for garnish

1. Place the cashews in filtered water in a small bowl. Cover and refrigerate overnight.
2. Lightly oil two 4-inch cheese molds with coconut oil.

3. In the bowl of a food processor, place the coconut and pulse until mealy in texture. Set aside.

4. Drain the cashews. In the pitcher of a Vitamix place the cashews, coconut, aquafaba, salt, and coconut oil. Blend on medium speed, using the plunger to evenly distribute the mixture until smooth.

5. You may need to stop the blender and scrape down the sides using a rubber spatula a few times.

6. Transfer the mixture to the prepared cheese molds. Cover the molds with parchment paper rounds cut to fit the molds.

7. Place the cheese molds in the dehydrator and dehydrate at 90 degrees F for 24 hours. Refrigerate overnight.

8. Remove the cheese from the molds. Arrange on plates and decorate with edible flower petals.

CONCLUSION

Cheese is a good source of calcium, a key nutrient for healthy bones and teeth, blood clotting, wound healing, and maintaining normal blood pressure. ... One ounce of cheddar cheese provides 20 percent of this daily requirement. However, cheese can also be high in calories, sodium, and saturated fat. Cheese is delicious as well!!

There's is also growing evidence indicating that eating a small amount of cheese after a meal can potentially help to prevent tooth decay and promote enamel re-mineralization. Not only does cheese contain a good amount of calcium, which supports strong and healthy teeth, cheese helps create additional saliva in your mouth, which helps whisk away food particles stuck to your teeth so they do not have a chance to settle in and cause staining. Hard cheeses, such as cheddar, are the most effective, so add a 1 oz. piece after a meal that includes teeth-staining foods.

When made properly, homemade cheese is often times better for you than store bought or commercial cheeses because they don't contain as much preservatives or other harmful, artificial ingredients.So what are you waiting for?

Lightning Source UK Ltd.
Milton Keynes UK
UKHW020701310521
384670UK00006B/185